new steps in religious education

BOOK 2

Third Edition

Nelson Thornes
a Wolters Kluwer business

Michael Keene

Text © Michael Keene 2002

Original illustrations © Nelson Thornes Ltd 2002

The right of Michael Keene to be identified as author of this work has been asserted by him in accordance with the Copyright, Designs and Patents Act 1988.

All rights reserved. No part of this publication may be reproduced or transmitted in any form or by any means, electronic or mechanical, including photocopy, recording or any information storage and retrieval system, without permission in writing from the publisher or under licence from the Copyright Licensing Agency Limited, Saffon House, 6-10 Kirby Street, London EC1N 8TS

Any person who commits any unauthorised act in relation to this publication may be liable to criminal prosecution and civil claims for damages.

First edition published in 1991.
Second edition published in 1997.
Third edition published in 2002 by:
Nelson Thornes Ltd
Delta Place
27 Bath Road
CHELTENHAM
GL53 7TH
United Kingdom

07 08 09 10 / 10 9 8 7 6 5

A catalogue record for this book is available from the British Library

First edition ISBN 0-871402-38-7
Second edition ISBN 0-7487-3078-8
Third edition ISBN 978-0-7487-6458-7

Illustrations by Richard Morris
Edited by Melanie Gray
Page make-up by Clare Park

Printed in China by Midas Printing International Ltd.

Acknowledgements

The author and publishers wish to thank the following for permission to reproduce photographs and other copyright material in this book:

Trip pp 11 & 101; Trip / G Lawrence p 12; Trip / M Feeney p 13; Trip / I Genut pp 70 & 71; Trip / H Rogers pp 76 & 102; Trip / A Tovy p 96; Trip / A Farago p 97; Trip / Andes Press p 98; Trip / V Schwanberg p 99; Trip / J Sweeney p 107. All other photographs supplied by The Walking Camera.

Every effort has been made to contact copyright holders and the publishers apologise to anyone whose rights have been inadvertently overlooked and will be happy to rectify any errors or omissions.

The scripture quotations (except where specifically indicated in the text) are taken from the Holy Bible, New International Version®. Copyright © 1973, 1978, 1984 by International Bible Society. Used by permission of International Bible Society. 'NIV' and 'New International Version' are trademarks registered in the United States Patent and Trademark office by International Bible Society.

Throughout the series the terms BCE (Before Common Era) and CE (Common Era) are used instead of the more familiar BC and AD. However, in practice, they mean the same thing.

Contents

1 Christianity then and now — 4
Introduction — 4
The Day of Pentecost — 6
Peter and Paul — 8
Christianity conquers Rome — 10
Early Christian missionaries — 12
The Great Split — 14
The Reformation and afterwards — 16
The Christian Church today — 18

2 The holy books — 20
Introduction — 20
The Bible — 22
Putting the Bible together — 24
Translating the Bible — 26
In the Bible — 28
Using the Bible — 30
The Tenakh — 32
The Qur'an — 34
The Hindu scriptures — 36
The Guru Granth Sahib — 38
The Buddhist holy books — 40

3 Religious worship — 42
Introduction — 42
Christian worship — 44
The sacraments — 46
Holy Communion — 48
Church leaders — 50
Jewish worship — 52
Muslim worship — 54
Hindu worship — 56
Sikh worship (1) — 58
Sikh worship (2) — 60
Buddhist worship — 62

4 Holy people — 64
Introduction — 64
Christian saints — 66
Christian monks and nuns — 68
Jewish prophets — 70
Muslim imams — 72
Hindu sadhus — 74
Sikh Gurus — 76
Buddhist monks and nuns — 78

5 Religious symbols — 80
Introduction — 80
Christian symbols — 82
Jewish symbols — 84
Muslim symbols — 86
Hindu symbols — 88
Sikh symbols — 90
Buddhist symbols — 92

6 Holy places — 94
Introduction — 94
Jerusalem — 96
Christian holy places — 98
Makkah — 100
Hindu pilgrimages — 102
Amritsar — 104
Buddhist holy places — 106

Glossary — 108

1 Christianity then and now

Introduction

Jesus was a Jew. He lived just over 2000 years ago in the tiny land of Palestine, a country in the Middle East which is now called **Israel**. For a long time Palestine was under Roman control and when Jesus was born it was ruled over by Herod the Great, a Jew. The Romans had put Herod on the throne to rule for them and he did exactly as he was told. He was there mainly to keep the Jews under control and he did this very effectively. He was a cruel and ruthless king who ruled with a rod of iron.

Jesus

The Jewish people hated being under Roman control and asked God to send them a leader to set them free from all their enemies. They called this ruler the **Messiah** and many people believed at first that Jesus was this promised leader. Jesus, however, was far from being the warrior or earthly king they were expecting the Messiah to be. Instead, he grew up in an ordinary Jewish family and tried to show the people how to live through his own example and teaching. He was a spiritual teacher, not a military one.

For three years Jesus travelled around Palestine with his 12 disciples. He chose them to be with him and to take over his work when he had left the earth. The **Gospels** explain that Jesus spent much of this time teaching by telling **parables** – stories taken from everyday life which carry a spiritual message. During this time Jesus also argued with the Jewish religious leaders, cared for the poor who came to him and performed miracles to help them. These miracles showed the people that Jesus had power over nature, sickness and death.

Jesus built up a large following among the people and this disturbed the Jewish authorities. They saw him as a real threat to their own leadership and wanted to see him dead. Eventually it was Pontius Pilate, the Roman governor, who condemned Jesus to death. He saw Jesus as a threat to the Roman Empire. In about 29 CE the Romans crucified Jesus on a hill outside the city of **Jerusalem**. Christians throughout the world remember the death of Jesus each year on **Good Friday**.

The resurrection

Three days after he was crucified the Gospels tell us that God brought Jesus back from the dead. This event is known as the **resurrection** and it is the most important belief in the Christian faith. Christians celebrate it each year at **Easter**. The Gospels say that during the following 40 days Jesus appeared to his disciples, and to others, in and around Jerusalem before leaving the earth for the last time. Before this happened, however, Jesus told his followers that they must preach his message throughout the world. They, and those who came after them, were so successful in doing this that by the fourth century the Roman Empire was being ruled by a Christian emperor.

In this unit

In this unit you will read about the following:

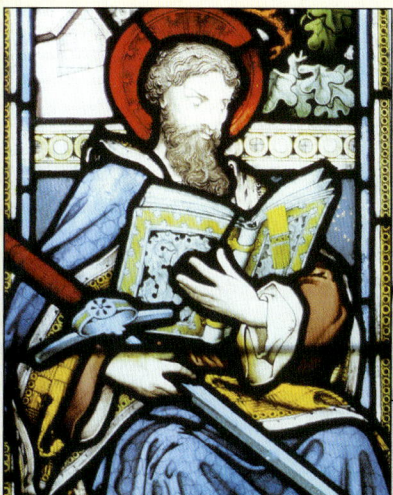

- The Day of Pentecost, the day on which the Christian Church was born. This day was marked by the giving of the **Holy Spirit** to the early Christians.

- **Peter** and **Paul**, the two most prominent leaders of the early Church. Paul took the Christian message through the Roman Empire and wrote many of the books in the **New Testament**.

- Some early Christian missionaries and the Great Split in the Church, which led to the formation of the **Roman Catholic Church** and the **Orthodox Church** in the eleventh century.

- The **Reformation** in the sixteenth century, which led to the birth of the **Church of England**. Later, **Nonconformist Churches** such as the **Baptist Church**, **Quakers** and **Methodist Church** were formed by people who also left the Church of England.

- The work in the Christian Church today of the **Salvation Army** and the London City Mission. Both these organisations work largely among the poorest people in the community.

Paul describes Jesus

Paul, the greatest leader of the early Christian Church, described Jesus as follows:

Who, being in very nature God... made himself nothing, taking the very nature of a servant, being made in human likeness. And being found in appearance as a man, he humbled himself and became obedient to death – even death on a cross!

In the glossary

Baptist Church	Orthodox Church
Church of England	Parables
Easter	Paul
Good Friday	Peter
Gospels	Quakers
Holy Spirit	Reformation
Israel	Resurrection
Jerusalem	Roman Catholic Church
Messiah	
Methodist Church	Salvation Army
New Testament	
Nonconformist Churches	

1 Christianity then and now

The Day of Pentecost

The story of what happened in Jerusalem soon after Jesus had left the earth is told in the Acts of the Apostles in the New Testament. The Acts of the Apostles is the only account we have of the birth and early years of the Christian Church. It was written by Luke, who also wrote one of the Gospels.

The Day of Pentecost

After Jesus had left them, his disciples gathered together in a room in Jerusalem to support each other. They felt alone and frightened. They did not know how to continue the work Jesus had started. They were frightened that the Romans would come at any time to arrest them. However, God's Holy Spirit came to them and they began to speak in different languages – the languages spoken by the people around them. You can read Luke's description of this event in the box on the next page.

The reason for the disciples speaking in many languages soon became clear. At this time people from many different countries had gathered in Jerusalem for the important Jewish festival of Pentecost. The disciples were now able to tell them about Jesus in their own words. You can see the countries these people came from in map A.

The visitors returned home after the festival had finished. Many of them believed the message that they had heard and become followers of Jesus. Through them the message began to spread well beyond the city of Jerusalem and out into the Roman Empire. The work of preaching the Christian message remains important for the Church today.

Understanding the events

Christians do not agree about what happened on the Day of Pentecost. There are some people who think the events took place just as Luke has described them. Others insist that Luke was simply using the symbols of fire and wind to convey something of the excitement and confusion of the event. All Christians agree, however, that this event marked the beginning of the Christian Church. From this moment onwards the very disciples who had been terrified by recent events went out fearlessly to preach the Christian message.

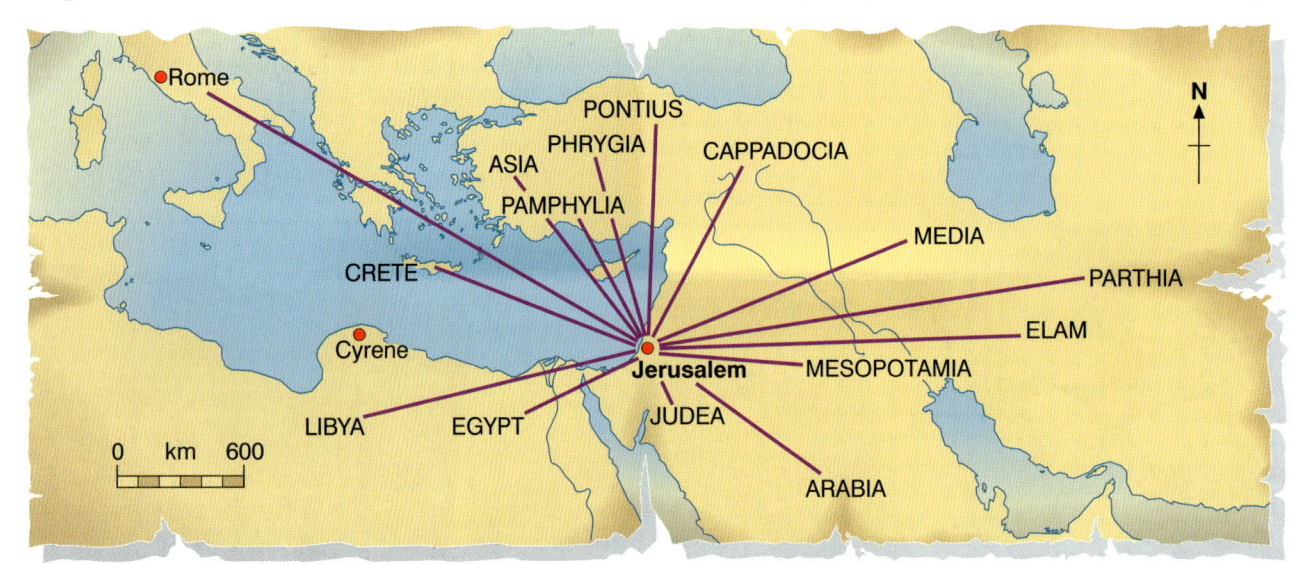

A This map shows where some of the people who became Christians on the Day of Pentecost came from

Christianity then and now 1

B The Holy Spirit came down on the disciples on the Day of Pentecost

The first day of Pentecost

This is how Luke describes the events of the first day of Pentecost:
When the day of Pentecost came, they were all together in one place. Suddenly a sound like the blowing of a violent wind came from heaven and filled the whole house where they were sitting. They saw what seemed to be tongues of fire that separated and came to rest on each of them. All of them were filled with the Holy Spirit and began to speak in other tongues, as the Spirit enabled them. Now there were staying in Jerusalem God-fearing Jews from every nation under heaven. When they heard this sound, a crowd came together in bewilderment, because each one of them heard them speaking in their own language.

Find the answers

- How were the disciples feeling when the events of Pentecost took place?
- Why were the disciples given the ability to speak in many languages?
- Why were these events so important in the history of the Christian Church?

Extra activity

In which ways would Christians say that the Holy Spirit is at work in the world today?

Learning about, learning from

1. Copy map A into your exercise book or file. Using an atlas, find out the modern names for three of the places labelled.

2. Why do you think the power of God is described as being like wind and fire?

3. Imagine you are an early Christian disciple who has been shattered and disillusioned by the death of Jesus.
   a. Describe the impact that the resurrection of Jesus and the giving of the Holy Spirit has had on you.
   b. Write down five words that most accurately describe your impression of what happened on the Day of Pentecost.

1 Christianity then and now

Peter and Paul

Peter and Paul were the most important leaders in the early Christian Church. Peter had been the leading disciple of Jesus and Paul was converted to Christianity in the early days of the Church.

Peter

Peter was born in the small fishing port of Bethsaida on the shores of Lake Galilee. His fisherman father called him Simon but Jesus renamed him Peter ('the rock') after he was chosen to be a disciple. Jesus said that Peter would be the 'rock' on which the Christian Church would be built. He soon became the leading disciple who was often able to understand important spiritual truths that the other disciples failed to notice. He was, for example, the first disciple to recognise that Jesus was God's Messiah.

Peter was one of the first people to see Jesus after his resurrection and he became the leader of the early Church. Roman Catholics believe that Peter was the first **Bishop** of Rome – the **Pope**. It seems that Peter was crucified by the Emperor Nero in 64 CE. The story says that Peter insisted on being crucified upside-down because he was not worthy to die in the same way as Jesus.

Paul

Paul was a Roman citizen and originally a Pharisee – a member of a strict Jewish religious group. The Pharisees strongly opposed Jesus during his lifetime and continued this opposition after his death. Paul led this opposition to the Christians until he was converted and became one of them himself. After he became a Christian, Paul dedicated the rest of his life to travelling throughout the Roman Empire as a missionary, preaching about Jesus. During these travels Paul's life was very eventful and included:

- being put into prison and flogged more than once
- being seized by a mob and almost lynched before Roman soldiers saved him
- being shipwrecked on his way to Rome to stand trial.

You can find out more about Paul's extraordinary travels by reading the letter in the box on the next page.

During his travels Paul founded many churches and some of the letters he later wrote to them are contained in the New Testament. He wrote a few letters to individual Christians, which are also included in the New Testament. The letters of Paul were highly prized by the early Christians. They are the oldest Christian documents we have, being written well before the Gospels. We are not sure how Paul died but it is likely he was beheaded at around the time that Peter was crucified. As a Roman citizen he could not be crucified.

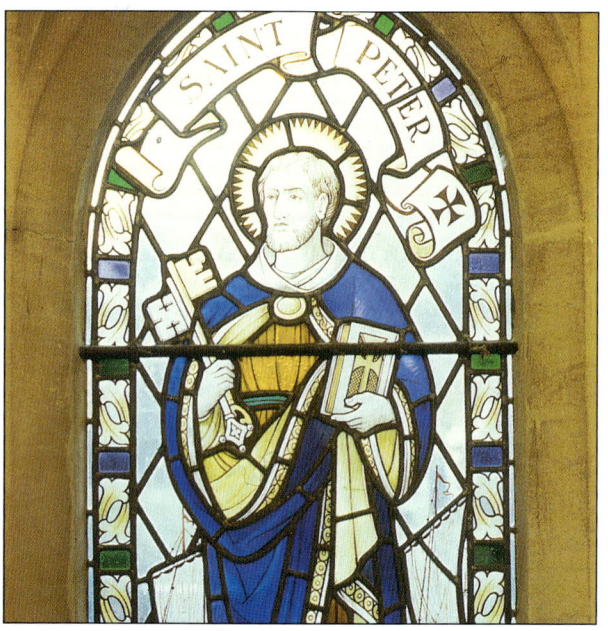

A Peter was the leader of the early Christian Church

Christianity then and now 1

B Paul was a tireless leader of the Church, whose writings are found in the New Testament

A difficult life

In one of his letters Paul describes the trials and tribulations that he went through:

Five times I was given thirty-nine lashes by the Jews; three times I was whipped by the Romans; and once I was stoned. I have been in three shipwrecks, and once I spent twenty-four hours in the water. In my many travels I have been in danger from floods and from robbers, in danger from fellow-Jews and from Gentiles; there have been dangers in the cities, dangers in the wilds, dangers on the high seas and dangers from false friends.

In the glossary
Bishop   Pope

Find the answers
- Why was Simon's name changed by Jesus and what was it changed to?
- Who is believed by many Christians to be the modern successor of Peter?
- What was Paul before he became a Christian?

Learning about, learning from

1. Picture A shows Peter holding the keys to heaven and hell. Read the background to this in Matthew 16.13–20 before answering the following questions.
   a. Who did the people think Jesus was?
   b. Who did Peter recognise Jesus to be?
   c. Who did Jesus say had revealed this truth to Peter?
   d. What did Jesus promise Peter?

2. a. Why do people need leaders?
   b. Which qualities make someone a good leader?
   c. Why were Peter and Paul good Christian leaders?

3. Why was Paul willing to go through so much to tell the people about Jesus and his teachings?

Extra activity
Find out more about a modern leader, such as Nelson Mandela or Desmond Tutu, and explain why people are willing to follow them.

1 Christianity then and now

Christianity conquers Rome

Peter and Paul were not the only missionaries in the early Church who tried to spread the Christian message. One disciple of Jesus, Thomas, is believed to have reached India. Other unknown followers helped to spread the message by talking about their faith wherever they went. You can see how quickly Christianity spread by looking at map A.

Persecution

From time to time the early Christians were persecuted. Some of the Roman emperors tried to wipe out the Christian religion entirely, believing it to be a threat to the Empire over which they ruled. Nero, who ruled between 54 CE and 68 CE, was one such ruler. In 64 CE he blamed the Christian community for a great fire in the city of Rome, which he himself had actually started! He rounded up thousands of Christians, nailed them to posts along the drive leading to his palace and set fire to them. No one knows exactly how many people died at his hands, or how many were put to death by other emperors.

Constantine's conversion

At the start of the fourth century everything suddenly changed. Constantine was involved in a bitter struggle with a rival over who should become emperor. Constantine prayed to the 'Supreme God' to help him in his struggle. The response was a sign – a cross in the sky with the words 'Conquer by this'. That night Constantine claimed that Christ appeared to him in a dream and told him to place the 'sign of the cross' at the head of his army. Constantine did as he was told and his army won against all the odds. The new emperor made sure the Christian religion was recognised officially throughout the Roman Empire. The days of Roman persecution for the Christian Church were over. Sunday became a day of rest throughout the Empire. This day had previously been devoted to the worship of a Roman god. Christians stopped observing the old Jewish day of rest, the **Sabbath Day**, and started meeting together on **Sunday**, the day on which Jesus had risen from the dead.

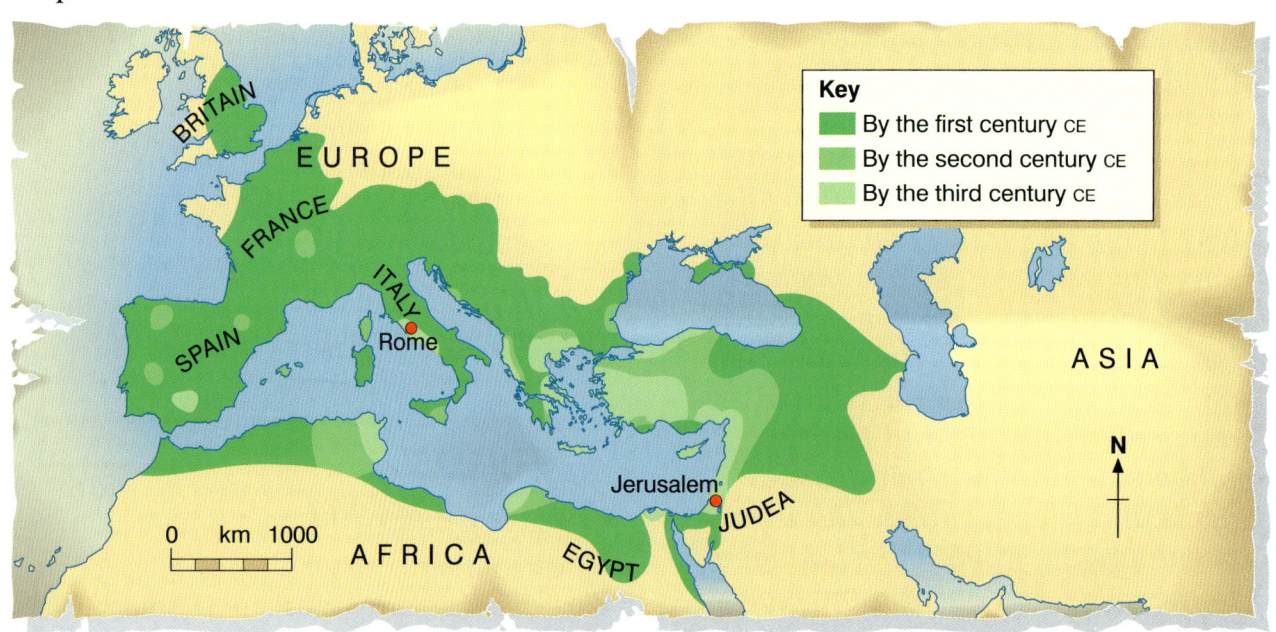

A This map shows the spread of the Christian message in the early years of the Church's existence

Christianity then and now 1

However, after Constantine died the Roman Empire was showing signs of crumbling. In less than a century its armies had withdrawn from most parts of the Empire before, at the start of the fifth century, they disappeared altogether. The almighty power of Rome was soon to be a distant memory. Christianity, however, did not die with the Roman Empire.

B Constantine was the first Roman emperor to recognise Christianity

In the glossary

Sabbath Day   Sunday

Find the answers

- Which disciple of Jesus is thought to have preached in India?
- What revenge did Nero take on the Christians for the fire in Rome?
- Who was the first Christian Roman emperor?

Tacitus speaks

Tacitus, a Roman historian who lived during the reign of Nero, describes the persecution of the Christians:

First those who confessed to being Christians were arrested. Then, on information obtained from them, hundreds were convicted more for their anti-social beliefs than for fire-raising. In their deaths they were made a mockery. They were covered in the skins of wild animals, torn to death by dogs, crucified or set on fire – so that when darkness fell they burned like torches in the night. Nero opened up his own gardens for this spectacle and gave a show in the arena, where he mixed with the crowd, or stood dressed as a charioteer on a chariot.

Learning about, learning from

1. Why was Constantine's conversion to Christianity so important for that religion?
2. Imagine you are a Christian at the time of Nero. The emperor has been rounding up your friends and putting them to death. Keep a diary for three days in which you describe your thoughts and feelings as you expect Roman soldiers to arrive and arrest you at any time.

Extra activity

Read the words of Tacitus in the box. Why do you think the early Christians aroused so much hatred and hostility in the Roman Empire? Does this hostility surprise you?

1 Christianity then and now

Early Christian missionaries

No one is quite sure how or when the new religion of Christianity first arrived in Britain. Probably some of the Roman soldiers who were sent to Britain when it was a distant outpost of the Empire were Christian believers. If so, we do not know their names or where they lived. Christianity, though, was probably in the country, and making converts, by the second century.

St Ninian and St Patrick

St Ninian has been described as 'the first and the greatest of the ancient Christian missionaries', yet we know very little about him. We do know, however, that he worked among the Picts in east Scotland and built a monastery at Whitehorn.

More is known about St Patrick (389–461 CE). At the age of 16 he was kidnapped from his father's farm in the west of England and taken to Ireland. During his six years of captivity there his faith in God grew. Until then religion had meant little to him but, as a captive of people who had no faith in God, his own prayers became important to him:

> Day by day as I went, a shepherd with my flock, I used to pray constantly... a hundred prayers a day, and nearly as many at night, staying out in the woods or on a mountain. And before daybreak I was up for prayer, in snow or frost or rain.

One night a voice spoke to Patrick in a dream telling him his ship was ready. He managed to escape and walked more than 300 kilometres to the nearest port. He arrived back in England, only to hear in his mind the voices of the people of Ireland begging him to return and walk among them. In 432 CE Patrick returned to spend the last 30 years of his life in Ireland.

Although not well educated himself, Patrick encouraged learning and built many monasteries. Many miracles were associated with his work. On one occasion he is said to have ordered frogs and vermin out of a village before banishing them to the marshes.

St Columba

Ireland was the birthplace of St Columba (521–597 CE), who became a famous abbot (head of a monastery) and missionary. In 563 CE, together with 12 friends, he set out from the Irish shores to undertake a pilgrimage. The pilgrimage took the party to Iona on the western coast of Scotland. There, Columba established a monastery

A St Patrick was an important early Christian missionary and started to preach to people who knew nothing about the Christian faith. Iona was to remain Columba's headquarters for the next 34 years while he and his followers converted a large part of western Scotland to Christianity. Since the 1930s Iona has been one of the most important destinations for Christian pilgrims.

B Iona is one of the most important pilgrimage sites for Christians today

The life of St Columba

This extract is taken from a biography of St Columba written in the seventh century:

From boyhood he had given himself as a Christian recruit to studies in quest of wisdom... God bestowed on him a sound body and a pure mind... he was angelic in appearance, bright in speech, holy in deeds, excellent in gifts and great in counsel. He could not let an hour go past without applying himself to prayer, reading, writing or some sort of work... he was dear to everybody, always showing a cheerful, holy face.

Find the answers

- Who was called 'the first and greatest of the ancient Christian missionaries'?
- Which missionary was called by God to work in Ireland?
- Which missionary founded a monastery on Iona?

Learning about, learning from

1. Write down three important facts about each of following.
   a. St Patrick.
   b. St Columba.

2. St Patrick only really discovered what he believed when he left home and lived among people who believed something different.
   a. What would you miss most if you moved to another country?
   b. What might you learn from your new surroundings?

3. What might people learn today from the life of St Patrick or St Columba?

Extra activity

There is almost always a miracle or more associated with the early Christian missionaries.
a. Why have such stories became associated with early missionaries, and what do they tell us about the way they were treated by others?
b. Would you expect miracles to be associated with holy people in the twenty-first century?

1 Christianity then and now

The Great Split

For some time the Christian Church was united, although its leaders often had differences of opinion. For example, in 49 CE Peter and Paul disagreed over whether Jews and Gentiles (non-Jews) were equal members of the Church. Then, in the third century, the Roman Empire was divided into eastern and western sections. In the fourth century Constantine, the Roman Emperor, set up a new capital city in the east, at Constantinople (now called Istanbul). After Rome was conquered by the Goths in 410 CE, Constantinople became the 'second Rome' and this had a great effect on the Church. The two parts, east and west, grew further apart. For example:

- Latin was spoken in the western Church centred on Rome
- Greek was spoken in the eastern Church centred on Constantinople.

There were other differences between the two parts of the Church. These focused on the various ways that the Christian faith was understood.

A Like the Orthodox Church, the Catholic Church also believes that its way of worshipping comes from the earliest days of the Christian Church

The Church begins to break up

A council of bishops meeting in 451 CE reached a conclusion that bishops from the east could not accept. According to Christians in the east, the great **Creeds** (statements of faith) of the Church could not be changed but those from the west wanted to alter them. The eastern churches thought this was unforgivable and the two parts of the Church began to drift apart. It was not until 1054, however, that the split finally came. This was brought about by the big question of how much authority the Pope should have. To Christians in the west he had the final word on everything, such as what people should believe and how they should worship. To Christians in the east the Pope was important but not that significant. For the first time in its history the Church split into two parts, the Roman Catholic Church and the Orthodox Church.

The Roman Catholic Church

The Roman Catholic Church was the western Church centred on the city of Rome, with the Pope as its leader. This Church, with over 1000 million members worldwide today, has always claimed to be the original Christian Church. It takes its authority from the teachings of Jesus and the original disciples. The Pope is seen to be the successor of Peter, the disciple of Jesus. The Roman Catholic Church has always been the largest of the Christian Churches and today 60 per cent of all Christians belong to it.

The Orthodox Church

The Orthodox ('right-thinking') Church is not a single Church but a 'family' of Churches which have much in common with each other. Although these Churches only came into existence after the Great

Split of 1054, they claim to represent the true Christianity which can be traced back to Jesus and his disciples. Although this Church was originally based in Constantinople, most Orthodox Christians are now found in Russia and Greece. The Orthodox Church takes its different names from the countries in which it is found. There are Greek, Russian, Serbian and Coptic Orthodox Churches, among many others – although recent steps have been taken to draw them much closer together.

B The Orthodox Church believes that its beliefs and worship go back to the time of the disciples of Jesus

The Church

Both the Roman Catholic and the Orthodox Churches believe that the Church is very important. This is what two Creeds say about it:
I believe in the holy catholic church, the communion of saints...
We believe in one holy, catholic [universal] and apostolic [based on the teachings of the apostles] church.

Christianity then and now 1

In the glossary
Creeds   Saints

Find the answers
- What was the name of the new city that Constantine set up in the east?
- What is a Creed?
- Which two Churches were formed after the Great Split?

Learning about, learning from

1 a. What was the issue that finally caused the split between the eastern and western parts of the Church?
  b. Why do you think the issue caused such a big argument?

2 a. Do you think it was a good thing or a bad thing that the Christian Church began to break up?
  b. Would it be a good thing or a bad thing for the Church to be united today?

Extra activity

Both the Roman Catholic and the Orthodox Churches claim to represent the oldest and purest form of Christianity. Why is this claim so important to both Churches?

1 Christianity then and now

The Reformation and afterwards

A There are millions of Baptists in the world today

For several centuries it seemed that matters had settled down but dissatisfaction was building up in the Roman Catholic Church. Matters came to a head in 1517. In that year Martin Luther, a Catholic, nailed a list of 95 things he did not like about the Catholic Church to the door of his own **church**. A movement known as the Reformation had begun. The effects of this were serious for the Roman Catholic Church in particular and the Christian Church in general.

The Reformation

The protest begun by Martin Luther led to the birth of the **Protestant Church**. As its name suggests, it was mainly launched in 'protest' against many of the teachings and practices of the Roman Catholic Church. In particular, Luther and others were unhappy about the Catholic practice of selling indulgences. The Church sold indulgences to Catholic believers, which promised them they would either spend little time in purgatory when they died or enter straight into heaven. The Church did this particularly when it needed to raise money for itself. Luther was eventually excommunicated (expelled) from the Roman Catholic Church and churches based on his teachings were set up across Europe.

In England at this time King Henry VIII fell out with the Pope, who would not allow him to divorce his wife. As a result, the king set himself up as head of the Church in England instead of the Pope. It was not until the reign of his daughter, Elizabeth I, that all ties with the Roman Catholic Church were broken by the English Church. When this happened the Church of England became the established (official) Church in England. When Churches based on the teachings of the Church of England were set up in other countries they became part of the **Anglican Church**.

Then, from the seventeenth century onwards, groups of Christians began to feel unhappy about some of the teachings of the Church of England and they broke away to form Churches of their own. These Churches became known as Nonconformist Churches because they could not 'conform' to the teachings of the Church of England. These Churches are also called 'Free Churches' because they are 'free' from any control by the Church of England.

Nonconformist Churches

The first Nonconformist Church to be formed was the Baptist Church. Today this Church is a worldwide organisation with over 50 million members. It began when John Smyth gathered together a community of believers in Amsterdam after they had been expelled from London. Baptists believe in the **baptism** of adult

Christianity then and now

believers and not the baptism of babies. The Anglican and Roman Catholic Churches believe in baptising babies.

Later in the seventeenth century the Quakers were formed. The Quakers are a Nonconformist Church with a largely silent form of worship. Many of them emigrated to America in 1650 and settled in the area later known as Pennsylvania. Then, in the eighteenth century, the Methodist Church was formed based on the preachings of John Wesley, an Anglican clergyman. They were known as Methodists because of the 'methodical' way they organised their prayers and **Bible** study.

B A Methodist church service – the Methodist Church was formed because many people were dissatisfied with the Church of England

In the glossary

Anglican Church Church
Baptism   Protestant Church
Bible

Find the answers

- What did Martin Luther do to show that he thought the Roman Catholic Church was doing wrong?
- Who set himself up as head of the Church in England instead of the Pope?
- What is the Anglican Church?

Learning about, learning from

1 a. In your own words, explain what indulgences are.
   b. Why do you think Martin Luther thought indulgences were a bad thing?

2 a. What things in the world today do you disagree with? Write a list of five things you would like to change – they can be about the world, the environment, your school or anything else.
   b. What would you do to start to put right these five things?

3 Why do you think Baptists believe only adults should be baptised and not babies? What arguments do you think an Anglican might put forward to show that they do not agree with the Baptists?

Extra activity

Is it a strength or weakness that there are so many different Christian Churches? Think of two arguments in favour and two against.

1 Christianity then and now

The Christian Church today

Since the earliest days of the Christian faith missionaries have been important in spreading the Church's message. The early disciples of Jesus were missionaries and the Christian message reached England through their work. In more recent years, too, the missionary work of the Church has continued. The first modern missionary was William Carey, a Northamptonshire cobbler who left the shores of England to take the Christian message to India in 1792.

The Salvation Army and the London City Mission

The missionary work of the Church continues today. Each year many Christian men and women leave Britain to work in other countries in skilled jobs such as doctors, nurses, teachers and agricultural experts. They are modern-day missionaries. At the same time, many Christians also come to live in Britain from other countries to work as missionaries.

Two organisations which have been carrying out missionary work in Britain for many years are:

- *the Salvation Army*. This organisation began its work in 1880 and its distinctive uniform is now a familiar sight on the streets of cities in Britain and overseas. For well over 100 years it has run mission halls (**citadels**), soup kitchens, hostels for the unemployed and a rescue agency for people who have lost contact with home. The Salvation Army is quick to respond to homelessness, natural disasters and national emergencies. It employs over 6000 people in more than 100 different countries to carry forward its work.
- *the London City Mission (LCM)*. The LCM was set up in 1835 to help the poor and needy in England's capital city. Today it has 130 full-time and voluntary missioners active in London's markets, housing estates, shops, factories and theatres. The missioners

A Many Salvation Army citadels are social centres providing food and shelter for those in need

Christianity then and now 1

are there to show the love of Jesus in the places where people live and work.

Much of the Church's missionary work goes on outside traditional church buildings. Among other places the message is being spread in coffee bars, beach missions and Christian arts and music festivals. The largest of these festivals, Greenbelt, attracts 25,000 young people each year.

The Church overseas

In many countries of the world members of the Christian Church are allowed to worship freely. However, in some places their freedom is severely restricted. In some countries in North Africa, for example, the Church is not allowed to make new converts. In other parts, such as Central and West Africa, the situation is very different. Today there are more than 150 million Christians in this area, with new churches being founded all the time. The same is also true of many countries in South and Central America. In this part of the world many of the **priests** identify themselves with the many people who are poor and needy. Some priests become involved politically and lead protests against those who exploit the people.

B Many Christians today meet in small house-churches to worship

In the glossary
Citadels   Priests

Find the answers
- What is a missionary?
- What are Salvation Army mission halls called?
- Where in the world is the Christian Church not allowed to make converts?

Learning about, learning from

1 Write two sentences about each of the following.
   a. The Salvation Army.
   b. The London City Mission.

2 a. Why do almost all Christian missionaries now take a skill with them to other countries, such as teaching or nursing?
   b. Why do missionaries not simply go out to other countries to preach, as they did in the past?
   c. Which skills do you think are most demand in some of the poorest countries of the world?

Extra activity

In recent years the Christian Church has lost many members in Britain. The Church of England recently appointed someone to look into the reasons for this decline. Imagine you have just taken on this job. Put forward three ways in which you would try to increase the number of people going to church.

2 The holy books

Introduction

Each of the world's great religions has its own holy book or books, known as scriptures. These are writings – some of which are very old – which are believed to carry God's message and it is this that gives them their special authority for religious believers. Because of their importance, believers today treat their scriptures with the greatest respect and they usually play a central part in nearly all acts of worship.

Writing the scriptures

Some of the scriptures took a long time to write before they were collected together. The Bible, for example, took more than 1500 years to collect together, although the New Testament was written in less than 100 years. It took almost another 300 years before the Christian Church accepted the authority of the whole Bible.

Scriptures are treated as holy when people believe they have come from God. They are often called 'the word of God' to show that the very words themselves were God-given. To Muslims, for example, the **Qur'an** is the perfect record of the revelations given by **Allah** to **Muhammad**. The **Prophet** Muhammad passed on these revelations to other people during his lifetime and they were written down by others some time later.

Respecting the holy books

Writings that are believed to be the holy word of God are treated with the utmost respect. For example, in a Sikh **gurdwara** the **Guru Granth Sahib** is carried above the heads of the worshippers before being placed on the takht (throne), which is itself above the heads of everyone when they are sitting to worship. If anyone has a copy of the Guru Granth Sahib at home it must have a room to itself, just as it does in a gurdwara.

When a scroll of the **Torah** is removed from the **Ark** in a Jewish **synagogue** and placed on the bimah (raised platform) to be read, it can only be followed using a metal pointer (yad). No one is allowed to touch the Torah with their fingers. It is too holy and touching the scroll may damage it. When a scroll reaches the end of its useful life it is buried just as a human being is – it is never destroyed.

The teachings in the scriptures

The most important part of the scriptures is the teachings they contain. As in the past, believers today expect to hear God speaking to them through their scriptures. This is the reason why readings from the scriptures play an important part in public and private worship. People look to the scriptures for guidance in shaping the direction their lives take. At times of difficulty Sikhs, for example, read the whole of the Guru Granth Sahib aloud (called an **Akhand Path**), which takes about 48 hours, allowing God to speak to them through its words.

In this unit

In this unit you will read about the following:

- The Bible. The Bible includes the Jewish scriptures as well as books written by the early Christians. Christians use the Bible in their public and private worship.

- The sacred scriptures of Jews, Muslims, Hindus, Sikhs and Buddhists. Each religion has its own distinctive way of treating its holy books with great respect. An important part of that respect is the use to which the followers put their sacred scriptures.

In the glossary

Akhand Path
Allah
Ark
Gurdwara
Guru Granth Sahib
Muhammad
Prophet
Qur'an
Synagogue
Torah

Studying the Torah

These words were written in the second century:

He who studies the Torah in order to learn and do God's will acquires many merits; and not only that, but the whole world is indebted to him. He is cherished as a friend, a lover of God and of his fellow men.

2 The holy books

The Bible

The Bible is the holy book of Christians. Reading the Bible is one of the most important ways for Christians to find out more about their faith. It also helps them to deepen their spiritual lives.

The Bible

The worldwide success of the Bible is very impressive. During the nineteenth and twentieth centuries over 3000 million copies of the Bible were sold. Each year a further 10 million is added to the total. There are now many different translations of the Bible available. Although the *Authorised Version* was first published in 1611, it is still popular. In recent years it has been overtaken, however, by more modern translations such as *The Good News Bible*, the *New International Version* and the *Revised English Bible*.

The Bible is divided into two sections:

- The **Old Testament**. The first part of the Christian Bible contains 39 books and is the sacred scriptures, or the **Tenakh**, of the Jews. The books of the Old Testament were written over a period of some 1000 years and it is not known who wrote most of them. They form the background to much of the New Testament and help Christians to understand this part of the Bible.
- The New Testament. The second part of the Bible is mainly concerned with the life and teaching of Jesus, the Messiah, whose coming into the world was prophesied in the Old Testament. In the New Testament there are two kinds of books:
  - History. The most important books in the New Testament are the four Gospels – Matthew, Mark, Luke and John. They are called Gospels – which means 'good news' – because they tell us about the life and teaching of Jesus who, Christians believe, brought 'good news' about the way God expects people to behave. The first three Gospels have a similar approach to telling this story but the fourth, John's Gospel, is very different and was written much later than the others. Luke, who was a doctor, not only wrote a Gospel but also the Acts of the Apostles. This book tells the story of the early days of the Christian Church after Jesus had left the earth.
  - Letters. There are many of these in the New Testament. They were written to help and encourage the early Christians. Most of the letters were written by Paul, although Peter and John also wrote some short ones.

Inspiration

At least 40 different authors wrote the 66 books in the Bible. Christians, however, see the Bible as one book rather than a collection of books. The writers of the different books, they believe, were all inspired by God in some way. Christians therefore believe that the Bible has an authority that no other book has.

A Worshippers in a Greek Orthodox church kiss the Bible to show their great respect for it

The holy books 2

B This stained-glass window reminds worshippers that the Bible is a very old book

From the Bible

These two verses from the New Testament refer to the Old Testament but they sum up what many Christians feel about the Bible as a whole:

We know that what the Scriptures say is true for ever... The word of God [the Bible] is living and active. Sharper than any two-edged sword, it penetrates even to the dividing of soul and spirit, joints and marrow; it judges the thoughts and attitudes of the heart.

In the glossary
Old Testament   Tenakh

Find the answers
- Which part of the Bible do Christians and Jews share?
- What is one difference between the Old and New Testaments?
- Which two kinds of writing go to make up the New Testament?

Learning about, learning from

1. Why might a Christian tell you that the Bible is a very important book to him or her?

2. a. What does the word 'Gospel' mean?
   b. Why were the four accounts of the life of Jesus called Gospels?

3. Although some ten million copies of the Bible are sold each year, not many people seem to actually read it. Explain why you think this may be.

Extra activity

The Bible was written many hundreds of years ago and by people living in a world very different to ours. Yet Christians believe its message is just as true today as when it was written. Do you agree that a book written so long ago can still be relevant today? Explain your answer.

2 The holy books

Putting the Bible together

Many of the passages in the Bible began life as stories, which had been kept alive for centuries by being passed down from one generation to another. However, as time went on, people began to write down this information so that it would not be forgotten. When **Moses**, for example, received the **Ten Commandments** on Mount Sinai, they are said to have been written on tablets of stone. These tablets were later stored, together with other holy objects, in a sacred box called the Ark. The ancient Jews took this box with them wherever they travelled. It was a constant reminder that God had spoken to them.

During the centuries that followed, when God spoke to the Jews through the many prophets he sent to them, their words were written down and kept. At about the same time many sacred songs, called psalms, were written down to be used in worship. There are 150 of these songs included in the Bible.

Bringing the books together

By the time of Jesus all the books of the Old Testament had been brought together. There was still a debate about one or two of them but the matter was finally settled at a meeting of **rabbis** in 90 CE. As most of the early Christians were Jews, they continued to use the Jewish scriptures in their worship.

At the same time, however, they talked about Jesus and his teaching. While they were still alive the disciples talked to the other followers of Jesus about him. They had travelled and listened to him. Some died as **martyrs** and there was a real fear that their memories of Jesus might die with them. To prevent this happening, in about 65 CE Mark wrote an account of the life of Jesus. This was about 35 years after Jesus was crucified. Matthew and Luke wrote their Gospels soon afterwards.

Each of them wrote their records on scrolls similar to those you can see in picture A. These were not, though, the earliest Christian books. Paul had already written many letters to the churches he had founded and the people he had met. Although Paul was not one of the original disciples of Jesus, he soon became the leader of the early Christians. His letters were treasured and read in many churches.

Gradually the letters of Paul and others were gathered together and added to the books of the New Testament. The Gospels were added later. One or two other books were also included. It was not until the fourth century, however, that the Church put its seal of approval on all these books and the Bible came into existence. Since then it has remained unchanged.

A This man is looking at the scrolls in the Ark of a synagogue

The holy books 2

B One of the followers of Jesus writes an account of his life and teaching

In the glossary
Martyrs Rabbis
Moses Ten Commandments

Learning about, learning from

1. **a.** Why did early Christians start to write down their memories of Jesus and his teaching?
   b. Why do you think Jesus did not write his own book about his message to the world?
   c. Paul's letters to the early churches are still an inspiration to many Christians today. Why are such ancient letters treasured by modern Christians?

2. The Gospels are not like a modern biography. Two descriptions of the same event often disagree about the details.
   a. In small groups, write down all you can remember from these two pages. Do not read them again!
   b. Compare what you have written with another group. Are there any differences or are both accounts exactly the same?
   c. Write a list of the main points from both accounts on one sheet of paper. Even if you think someone else's point is wrong you should include it.
   d. Do you think the people who decided what should go in the Bible were right to include all four Gospels, or should they have included just the one containing the most information?

Find the answers

- Who received the Ten Commandments on Mount Sinai and what were they written on?
- When were the books of the Old Testament brought together?
- Which books in the New Testament were the first to be written?

Extra activity

Many Christians believe that the words of the Bible were inspired by God, yet we know they were written down by people many years after the events they record. Write a short conversation between someone who thinks the words are still very special and someone who does not.

25

2 The holy books

Translating the Bible

The Old Testament was originally written in Hebrew and the New Testament in Greek. Towards the end of the fourth century Jerome translated the Bible into Latin and, for a long time, this was the only translation used in Britain. Sometimes, however, the English translation was written underneath the Latin words. A beautiful example of this is the Lindisfarne Gospels, which were produced by **monks** living on Holy Island, off the north-east coast of England.

Translating the Bible into English

In the fourteenth century John Wycliffe, a travelling preacher, argued that the Bible should be translated into English so that everyone could read it – only the local priest could read Latin. His followers started to translate the Bible, copying it out by hand. About 200 copies of their work still exist.

The first book was printed in 1454 but, surprisingly, the first English Bible was not printed until 1526. Even then it was only a copy of the New Testament and this proved to be highly controversial. It was the work of William Tyndale, who had to print it in Germany and smuggle copies into Britain to avoid being arrested. The Church leaders felt threatened by the thought of the people having the Bible in their own language and Tyndale was eventually burned at the stake in Belgium in 1536. However, two years later there was a copy of the English Bible in every church in England. To prevent thieves from taking it the Bible was usually chained down.

Modern versions

In 1611 the most famous English version of the Bible, the *Authorised Version*, was printed. It has never been out of print since and some Christians still use it today. For over 350 years this version reigned supreme although another edition, the *Revised Version*, was published in 1885. Much later J B Phillips, a young Anglican clergyman, found that young people in his church could not understand the Bible and he translated some of the books into modern English to help them. These translations proved to be very popular just after the Second World War.

In 1961 the *New English Bible* was published. This became popular for reading aloud in church services and it was revised in 1985 as the *Revised English Bible*. Nothing, however, can rival the success of the *Good News Bible*, which was published in America for people who use English as their second language. The language used was simple and, in its first year, over 8 million copies of the translation were sold – mainly to people whose *first* language was English. Today over 80 million copies of the *Good News Bible* are in circulation. Apart from its easy-to-read text, an added attraction was its unusual illustrations.

A The public reading of passages from the Bible is an important part of Christian worship

The holy books 2

B The Jewish scriptures were first written in Hebrew

The Lindisfarne Gospels

At the end of the Lindisfarne Gospels the monks involved in the translation added this note:
Eadfrith, Bishop of the Church at Lindisfarne, he at the first wrote this book for God and St Cuthbert and for all the saints in common that are on the island, and Ethilwald, Bishop of those of Lindisfarne Island, bound and covered as best he could. At Bilfrith the anchorite [hermit] he wrought as a smith the ornaments that are on the outside, and adorned it with gold and with gems, also with silver overgilded, a treasure without deceit. And Alfred, an unworthy and most miserable priest, with God's help and Cuthbert's, overglossed it in English.

In the glossary
Monks

Find the answers
- In which languages were the Old and New Testaments originally written?
- What are the Lindisfarne Gospels?
- Who lost his life for printing the first copy of the New Testament in English?

Learning about, learning from
1. Why might it matter to some people that only their priest, and not them, could read the Bible in Latin?
2. The Bible has been translated into many modern versions. Should the language of a holy book be brought up to date or not? Try to use the phrase 'the word of God' in your answer.

Extra activity
Why were the king and the religious authorities opposed to the Bible being translated and printed in the language of the people? What do you think they were worried about?

2 The holy books

In the Bible

The Bible falls into two parts – the Old Testament, which tells the history of the Jewish people, and the New Testament, which tells the story of Jesus and the early Christian Church.

The Old Testament – the history of Jews

The opening chapters of the first book of the Bible, Genesis, try to answer some important questions:

- Who created the world and how?
- Where did the first human beings come from?
- What is sin?
- What does God have to say to the human race?

According to Genesis the whole world was created in seven days, with the first man and woman – Adam and Eve – being placed by God in a perfect garden. Nothing disturbed their perfect world until sin entered. The woman gave in to the temptation of the serpent (snake) and persuaded her husband to do the same. God punished the man and the woman for their sins by banishing them both from the garden. In the harsh outside world the man had to work hard to provide for his family while the woman had to go through the pain of childbirth. Hard, physical work and painful birth are seen as divine punishments for human sin.

So begins the story that runs through the rest of the Old Testament. It was **Abraham**, the father of the Jewish nation, who made an agreement with God that his descendants would worship God alone. Abraham's grandson, Jacob, was renamed Israel and his 12 sons became the fathers of the 12 tribes of Israel. The nation of Israel, the Jews, was born.

A The Bible begins with the story of the creation of the universe and of the first man and woman

Jews spent much time in slavery. God sent them many outstanding leaders, including Moses, but each time the Jews failed to live up to the teaching that God gave them. In the end they lost their homeland, Israel, and, as the Old Testament ends, they were under Roman control.

The New Testament – Jesus and the Church

Then came Jesus. His followers believed he was God's Son, the Messiah, the chosen leader of the Jews. As an adult he was baptised by John the Baptist in the River Jordan. For a short time Jesus taught his disciples and the people about God before he was put to the death by the Roman

The holy books 2

authorities who saw him as a threat. The New Testament tells us that shortly after being buried Jesus was brought back to life by God – an event known as the resurrection. This belief is the most important one in Christianity.

The Gospels and the other writings in the New Testament explain the meaning of these events to Christian believers. Paul's letters were sent to individual Christians as well as churches, setting out what it means to be a Christian. Strangely, though, Paul and other writers in the New Testament rarely refer to actual events in the life of Jesus.

B To Christians, the most important event in the Bible is the returning of Jesus to life after his crucifixion

In the glossary
Abraham

Find the answers
- What are the names of the two parts of the Bible?
- Whose history is recorded in the Old Testament?
- How were the first man and woman punished for their sins?

Learning about, learning from

1. **a.** If you had never read the Bible, what would you expect to find in it?
   b. Why do you think the Bible contains the story of both Jews and Christians?
   c. How might people today find the stories in the Bible useful in their everyday lives?

2. Design a poster to be displayed in your school showing people what is in the Bible.

3. Read the story of the first man and woman in the Garden of Eden in Genesis 3. Can you find anything in the story which would be useful for people to learn today?

Extra activity
Sum up, in just three sentences, the message of the Bible.

2 The holy books

Using the Bible

The Bible plays an important part in the lives of Christians, as well as being at the heart of worship in church. It plays a central part in three aspects of Christian life: in personal Bible study, at Bible study meetings and at Bible readings in church.

Personal Bible study

Most Christians want to know and understand their Bible better. Many set aside some time each day when they pray and read the Bible. They believe God can speak to them through the words of the Bible and they pray beforehand that this will happen. For this to happen, they ask that God's Holy Spirit will help them to understand what they are reading.

Many Christians use Bible study notes to help them understand the meaning of the Bible passage they are reading. If used daily, some notes will lead them through the whole Bible in about three years. There are different notes which are suitable for children, young people and adults.

Bible study with others

Most church congregations provide the opportunity for members to meet in small groups and these meetings are usually held in someone's house. It is at these meetings that a passage from the Bible is discussed, usually under the leadership of someone experienced in Bible study. In the Anglican and Roman Catholic Churches this kind of Bible study is often part of preparation for Easter during the time of **Lent**. This is the time when Christians return to the story of the death and resurrection of Jesus in the Gospels and spend time thinking, praying and reflecting on it.

Bible reading in church services

Passages from the Bible are read aloud in almost all church services. In the Anglican and Roman Catholic Churches there are three readings during most services:

- A reading from the Old Testament.
- A passage from the Gospels.
- A reading from the letters of the New Testament (**Epistles**).

The readings are given from the lectern at the front of the church. The readings from the Old Testament and the Epistles can be given by a member of the congregation but the one from the Gospels is usually given by the priest. This sometimes takes place in the middle of the church, with the Bible being held up by a server. This mark of respect emphasises the belief that the reading from the Gospels is central to worship and is taken from the most important part of the scriptures.

Although the **sermon** is a part of almost all worship, it is particularly important in

A In many churches a Bible is left open to show people that the church is based on its teachings

The holy books 2

Nonconformist Church worship such as the Baptists or the Methodists. This is the part of the service where the priest or **minister** explains some part of the Bible to members of the congregation.

In the glossary
Epistles   Minister
Lent   Sermon

Find the answers
- In which Churches is a study of the Bible most likely to be a part of the season of Lent?
- From where is the Bible usually read in a church service?
- Why might the Gospels be read from the centre of the church during a service?

B Many Christians take time out each day to read and study the Bible

Learning about, learning from
1. **a.** On which occasions might a Christian hear the Bible being read in public?
   b. What might a Christian hope to hear as they listen to the Bible being read?
2. Most Christians are anxious to grow spiritually in their Christian lives. How do you think they might use the Bible to help them to do this?
3. **a.** During church services why are passages taken from the Old Testament, the Gospels and the New Testament?
   b. Why is it only the priest, in some churches, who reads the passage from the Gospels?

Extra activity
Christians believe that the Bible cannot simply be read like any other book – it needs to be studied and thought about. Most churches have someone like a priest to explain the meaning of the Bible. Does this mean that reading the Bible in church might be more effective than reading the Bible at home? How do you think a Christian might answer this question?

2 The holy books

The Tenakh

The Tenakh is the name given to the Jewish scriptures. It is a collection of books written in Hebrew by many different authors over a long period of time. Some of the same books form the Old Testament of the Christian Bible. Originally the Tenakh was written on parchment scrolls and this is how the Torah, the first five books of the Tenakh, is preserved today. Each modern scroll is copied out by a scribe and must be perfect. A single mistake and the work must begin again.

The Jewish scriptures are divided into three parts: the Torah, the Nevi'im and the Ketuvim.

The Torah (the Five Books of Moses)

This includes the first five books of the Bible – Genesis, Exodus, Leviticus, Deuteronomy and Numbers. These books contain the story of how the ancient Israelite nation spent over 400 years in Egyptian slavery before being freed by God working through Moses. The account ends 40 years later with the Israelites entering the Promised Land of Canaan, later to become the land of Israel. During the journey from Egypt to Canaan, called the **Exodus**, the Jewish people received their laws from God on Mount Sinai, including the Ten Commandments. These laws are at the heart of the Torah. Jews today still try to follow them as the basis for their everyday lives. They regard the Torah as God's most precious gift to the Jewish nation.

The Nevi'im (the Books of the Prophets)

The prophets were men and women who spoke to the people on God's behalf. These books contain the moral and religious teachings of these people. Among the most important prophets were Isaiah, Ezekiel and Jeremiah. Although the prophets sometimes spoke of events in the future, they were much more concerned with how people should live each day.

The Ketuvim (the Writings)

This is a collection of poetry, proverbs and other writings by such important Jewish leaders as David and Solomon. Jews regard these books as holy but not as important as the Torah and the Nevi'im.

The scrolls

When a new Torah scroll is presented to a synagogue a special ceremony takes place. It is then put into the Ark with the other scrolls after it has been 'dressed' and capped with a silver crown. During services the scrolls are brought out of the Ark and carried in procession to the bimah, the ledge across the front of the synagogue. The scrolls are then 'undressed' and the relevant passage is read.

A In some synagogues only men are allowed to read the scriptures in public, but in others women can do so as well

The holy books 2

B The scrolls of the Torah are stored in the Ark in the synagogue

The Torah

In 132 CE the Roman emperor, Hadrian, forbade all Jews to study or teach the Torah. Rabbi Akiva refused to obey the order. He said:
A fox once called the fishes in a stream to come ashore and escape from the big fish that preyed on them. They told him that water was their life-element; if they left it they would surely die. If they stayed some might die but the rest would live. The Torah is our element of life. Some of us may perish in the trials of these days but as long as there is Torah the people will live.

In the glossary
Exodus

Find the answers
- What is the name given to the Jewish scriptures?
- Into which three parts are the Jewish scriptures divided?
- Where are the Jewish scrolls kept in a synagogue?

Learning about, learning from

1 a. Describe the ways in which the Torah is treated with great respect in a synagogue.
   b. Why is the Torah treated in this way?

2 Jews are taught that it is better to study than to pray. The study of the Torah always takes place in pairs. Why do you think this is?

3 Read the extract about the Torah in the box.
   a. What did Rabbi Akiva mean when he told this story?
   b. What, if anything, do you have which is more important to you than life itself?

Extra activity
a. The Torah is called 'the Tree of Life' in Judaism. Explain why it is so called.
b. An old Jewish story says that there was complete silence on the earth when God gave the Torah to Moses. What point do you think this story is making?

2 The holy books

The Qur'an

The Qur'an is the holy book for all Muslims. The name comes from the Arabic word meaning 'that which is read or recited'. It contains all the revelations given by Allah to the Prophet Muhammad.

Putting the Qur'an together

Muslims believe there are two perfect copies of the Qur'an. One is in heaven and the other is the one that the followers of Muhammad put together after the Prophet's death. It was written in three stages:

1. During many revelations the Angel Jibril (Gabriel) told Muhammad about the will and mind of Allah. Muhammad was in a cave in Hira when the angel came to him.
2. For many years afterwards Muhammad was followed by a growing group of companions. They made a note of the revelations Muhammad had received by writing them down on fragments of stone, pieces of palm branches or whatever else came to hand.
3. A few years later, after Muhammad's death, his friends decided to bring this material together to make a permanent record. Four copies of the Qur'an were made and sent to cities where there were many Muslim converts.

B When the Qur'an is not being read it is treated with the greatest possible respect

A Boys learn Arabic from an early age so that they can read the Qur'an and understand what it is saying

The words of the Qur'an

The words of the Qur'an have never been changed since they were first revealed to Muhammad. The language of the Qur'an is Arabic, which sounds particularly beautiful when it is read aloud. The text itself reads from right to left on the page and starts at the top right-hand corner. Although the Qur'an has been translated into many languages, it is best read in Arabic. Muslim children start to learn this language at the age of four in the madrasah, a special school attached to the **mosque**.

In total the Qur'an has over 6000 verses. A verse is called an ayah or 'sign'. These verses are divided into chapters or surahs ('steps up'), and each chapter has its own title. The title describes the most important theme in the surah.

Respecting the Qur'an

Muslims treat the Qur'an with the greatest respect. Before reading it they wash themselves thoroughly. They unwrap the

The holy books 2

holy book from its cover, read the passage and replace it carefully on the shelf. It is important that the Qur'an is stored higher than any other book. It is never placed on the floor and, when a Muslim is reading from it, the holy book is placed on a stand. While it is being read, people do not eat or drink, or behave in any way that shows a lack of respect.

C Although Muslims regularly read the Qur'an, they spend longer studying it at special times of the year such as **Ramadan**

From the Qur'an

This Qur'an could not have been composed by any but Allah... It is beyond doubt from the Lord of Creation. If they say, 'It is your own invention', say 'Compose one chapter like it.'

In the glossary
Mosque   Ramadan

Find the answers
- If one perfect copy of the Qur'an is in heaven, where is the other one?
- How did Muhammad receive the revelations that make up the Qur'an?
- In which language was the Qur'an written?

Learning about, learning from

1. **a.** Why is the Qur'an placed high on a shelf when it is not being used?
   b. Which books do you value or respect most? How do you treat them?

2. **a.** Why do Muslims always treat the Qur'an with great respect?
   b. How do they do this?

3. What difference do you think it might make to your life if you were to spend some time each day reading a holy book like the Qur'an?

Extra activity

The following quotation comes from the Qur'an. Explain in two sentences what it means. 'This Qur'an will guide men to that which is most upright. It promises the believers who do good works a rich reward, and threatens those who deny the life to come with a grievous scourge.'

2 The holy books

The Hindu scriptures

There are many Hindu holy books and these are divided into two groups, the **Shruti** and the **Smriti**.

The Shruti ('what is heard')
The Shruti contain the four Vedas and the Upanishads, which explain the teachings of the Vedas. These are the oldest known books. The word 'Veda' means 'knowledge' and Hindus believe these books have come directly from God. Revealed originally to the holy men of India, the Vedas have been passed down for centuries. The Rig Veda, the most important of the Hindu scriptures, contains 1028 hymns to various Hindu gods.

The Smriti ('what is remembered')
These are holy writings other than the Vedas, which Hindus have remembered and passed on from generation to generation. Some Hindus believe Smriti are less important than Shruti, while to others they are of equal value.

The Mahabharata
The Purana and Itihasa are part of the Smriti scriptures and tell stories from Indian legends and history. Among them is the **Mahabharata**, which is the longest and oldest poem in any language. It has three million words and tells the story of two sets of royal cousins who quarrel over who should succeed to the throne. Finally they go to war. Arjuna, one of the cousins, hates fighting but is an excellent warrior. In the final battle Arjuna hesitates because he does not want to kill members of his own family. He orders his chariot driver to withdraw from the battle. Arjuna is surprised when his driver begins to argue with him. Then he realises that his driver is none other than the god **Krishna**, who has come to live on earth. Krishna tells Arjuna that those who die in battle are not dead for ever. The prince believes him and leads his forces to victory.

The Mahabharata also includes the ancient **Bhagavad Gita** – the Song of the Lord. Spoken by Krishna, this is one of the most important Hindu scriptures.

The Ramayana
The **Ramayana** is another great Hindu epic poem. It tells the story of Rama, a god, who visits earth and marries Princess Sita. She is abducted by Ravana, a fierce demon, and taken to the island of Lanka. After fierce fighting Rama rescues her and they are restored to their thrones.

The theme of both the Mahabharata and the Ramayana is also the theme of most stories in the Hindu scriptures – the struggle between good and evil in the world. Although evil sometimes appears to be winning the fight, it is always good that conquers in the end.

A Some of the Hindu scriptures are believed to have come directly from God and they are among the oldest known books

The holy books 2

B Some of the Hindu scriptures are those which have been passed down by word of mouth – these are sometimes considered to be less important than those which have come from God

The Laws of Manu

This extract comes from the Laws of Manu, a Hindu book written between 200 and 100 BCE:
Coveting [wanting] the property of others, thinking in one's heart of what is undesirable, and adherence [sticking] to false doctrines [beliefs] are three kinds of sinful mental action. Abusing others, speaking untruth, detracting from the merits of all men and talking idly shall be four kinds of evil verbal action.

In the glossary

Bhagavad Gita   Ramayana
Krishna   Shruti
Mahabharata   Smriti

Find the answers

- Which is the most important group of Hindu scriptures?
- What is the name of the longest poem in the world?
- Which Hindu holy book tells the story of the rescue of Sita by Rama?

Learning about, learning from

1 Match up the words in the left-hand column with their correct meaning in the right-hand column.

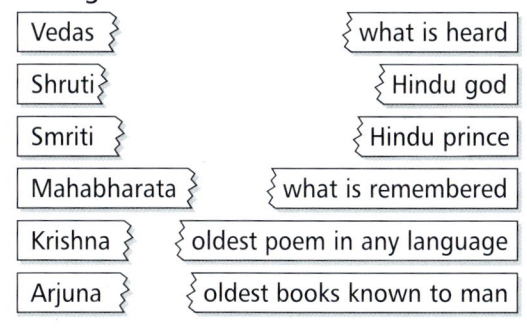

Vedas	what is heard
Shruti	Hindu god
Smriti	Hindu prince
Mahabharata	what is remembered
Krishna	oldest poem in any language
Arjuna	oldest books known to man

2 The Hindu holy books show that good always triumphs over evil in the world.
 a. Write down three things that you think are good in this world.
 b. Write down three things that you think are evil.
 c. Do you expect good to usually triumph over evil?

3 Read the extract from the Laws of Manu in the box. How do you think the words about truth and truthfulness could help people today? Give examples in your answer.

Extra activity

Explain why the Vedas in the Shruti are thought by many Hindus to be more important than the Smriti.

2 The holy books

The Guru Granth Sahib

In 1604 Guru Arjan collected together the teachings of the four **Gurus** (spiritual teachers) who had come before him. He combined them with many holy songs and poems written by Muslim and Hindu holy men to form the **Adi Granth**. By so doing he was illustrating the Sikh belief that truth is not to be found in just one religion because there are many paths to God.

Shortly before he died in 1708 the tenth and last Guru, **Guru Gobind Singh**, added the writings of his father to the Adi Granth to form the Guru Granth Sahib. He also told Sikhs that there would be no more human Gurus to lead them. From now on their only teacher would be the holy book.

The Guru Granth Sahib

For any building to be recognised as a gurdwara it must have a copy of the Guru Granth Sahib inside. The holy book, the symbol of God's presence, plays an important role in Sikh worship. Here are three examples:

- When young babies are brought into the gurdwara for the first time, the holy book is opened at random to provide the first letter of the baby's name.
- Marriages are performed in front of the book.
- Before a family moves into a new home, the Guru Granth Sahib is put into the new dwelling for an hour or so.

Respecting the Guru Granth Sahib

At the end of each day the Guru Granth Sahib is taken to a special room in the gurdwara. The room contains a bed covered with romallas (silk cloths). Everyone stands as the **granthi** recites the **Ardas** prayer and covers the holy book, and his own head, with clean cloths. The Guru Granth Sahib is carried to its overnight resting place on the granthi's head. Next morning it is returned to the takht (throne) in the gurdwara in the same way.

Anyone who will come into contact with the holy book must take a bath and wash his or her hands before turning its pages.

For a long time Sikhs resisted all attempts to have copies of the Guru Granth Sahib printed because they did not want it handled by non-Sikhs. Each copy of the Guru Granth Sahib must be an exact copy of the original and contain 1430 pages.

Some Sikh homes contain a copy of the Guru Granth Sahib, which must be placed in its own room (called a gurdwara). Many families, however, cannot give the holy book a room of its own. In these homes the family has a copy of the Gutka, a shorter book containing extracts from the Guru Granth Sahib.

The Mool Mantar

The most important passage in the Guru Granth Sahib comes at the beginning. It is the Sikh Creed or statement of belief – the **Mool Mantar**. You can read this in the box on the next page. The Mool Mantar is the opening section of the Japji, the morning prayer recited each day by all Sikhs.

A Someone often sits behind the Guru Granth Sahib waving a fan made of yak hair or nylon

The holy books 2

B A building is only recognised as a gurdwara when a copy of the Guru Granth Sahib is in place there

The Mool Mantar

There is One God Whose Name is Truth,
God is the Creator, and without fear and without hate.
God is timeless.
God's Spirit is throughout the universe.
God is not born, Nor will die to be born again, God is self-existent.
By the grace of the Gurus God is made known to mankind.

In the glossary

Adi Granth
Ardas
Granthi
Gurus
Guru Gobind Singh
Mool Mantar

Find the answers

- Who compiled the Adi Granth?
- What is the difference between the Adi Granth and the Guru Granth Sahib?
- What makes a building a gurdwara?

Learning about, learning from

1. Write down three ways in which Sikhs show great respect for their holy book.

2. a. What is the Mool Mantar?
   b. Where would you find it in the Guru Granth Sahib?
   c. List three things that a Sikh learns about God from the Mool Mantar.

3. The Sikh religion says that the Guru Granth Sahib is a teacher and leader. Is this different from how other religions view their holy books? What are the similarities and differences?

Extra activity

It has been said that Sikhs honour the Guru Granth Sahib without worshipping it. What do you think this means?

39

2 The holy books

The Buddhist holy books

It was not until 500 years after the death of the **Buddha** in 483 BCE that his teachings were written down. In those days people kept information alive for long periods of time by word of mouth. However, to make sure that everyone agreed on what the Buddha had actually said, gatherings of monks listened to all his teachings being recited by two of his closest followers. Since the Buddha's death such meetings had been held regularly to make sure that the memory of his teachings was still reliable.

The Pali and Sanskrit Canons

Two collections of the Buddha's teachings were made. These are called the Pali Canon and the Sanskrit Canon after the two ancient languages in which they were first written.

- The Pali Canon was the first to be put together and was written in an Indian language by the people of Sri Lanka. This took place in about 30 BCE. The Pali Canon is the most important collection of writings for **Theravada Buddhists**.
- The Sanskrit Canon, written in another ancient Indian language, is widely used by **Mahayana Buddhists**.

The three baskets

The Buddhist scriptures consist of a threefold collection of texts called the Tipitaka ('the three baskets'). They were probably called 'baskets' because the teachings were first written down on palm leaves and stored in baskets.

- Basket One is made up of the rules of discipline for Buddhist monks and **nuns**.
- Basket Two contains the actual teachings of the Buddha. It is called the Suttaka Pitaka ('sutta' means 'teaching'). This collection is widely read as an important account of what the Buddha said and did. The teachings are called the **Dhamma** and the most well known of these texts is the Dhammapada. You can read more about this in the box on the next page.
- Basket Three contains an explanation of the Buddha's teaching.

The Mahayana scriptures

Both Theravada and Mahayana Buddhists follow the teachings of the Tipitaka but they disagree over which is the most important. For Mahayana Buddhists, the Diamond Sutta and the Lotus Sutta are two of the most important parts. They also have their own holy books.

A The books considered to be holy by Buddhists fall into two groups – those holy to Mahayana Buddhists and those holy to Theravada Buddhists

In the glossary

Buddha
Dhamma
Mahayana Buddhists

Nuns
Theravada Buddhists

The holy books 2

B The purity of the Buddhist scriptures has been maintained by regular meetings of monks

From the Dhammapada

The Dhammapada is a collection of the Buddha's teachings. Here is an extract:

As the arrow-maker whittles
They tremble, they are unsteady,
And makes straight his arrows
They wander at their will
So the master directs
It is good to control them
His straying thoughts.
And to master them brings
Happiness.

Find the answers

- When did the Buddha die?
- How many collections of the Buddha's teachings were made and what are they called?
- What is the Tipitaka?

Learning about, learning from

1. a. How were the teachings of the Buddha first kept alive?
   b. When were the teachings first written down?
   c. How did his followers make sure that only a reliable account of the teachings was recorded?

2. Read the extract from the Dhammapada in the box.
   a. How does the master (spiritual teacher) direct his thoughts?
   b. What happens to our thoughts if we do not control them?
   c. How can a person find happiness?.

3. Buddhists do not believe in God, as do the other religions in this book. What, then, might be the purpose of their holy books?

Extra activity

There is a difference of opinion about which is the most important part of the Buddhist scriptures. If the three baskets contain the rules for Buddhist monks, the actual teaching of the Buddha and the explanation of the Buddha's teaching, which would you say was most important? Explain your answer.

41

3 Religious worship

Introduction

The feelings that religious people have for God are the deepest of all. They may even be deeper than the feelings they have for the closest members of their own family. They express these deep feelings each time they offer worship to God. In worship a person recognises that there is someone of much greater worth than themselves, and that this someone is God. It is these feelings that people express through their worship – whether they are in a church, synagogue, mosque, gurdwara, **mandir** or **temple**.

Religious worship

Although true worship means far more than the words people use and the actions they perform, words and actions are important. In worship people pray together, sing songs, give offerings to God, visit holy places and read holy books. Celebrating festivals is also an important part of religious worship, bringing together people with a common purpose to remember an important religious leader or a significant event in the past. There are many different aspects to religious worship.

People use these outward actions of worship, sometimes called 'rituals', as a way of expressing their inner spiritual feelings. Singing a song together, joining in a familiar prayer or presenting an offering to God all help people to express what they feel and believe about the world beyond this one – the spiritual world. Usually these actions have been hallowed (made holy) by centuries of use. For example, when Orthodox Christians celebrate their most important service, the **Divine Liturgy**, they are using words and actions that date back, almost unchanged, to the fourth century.

The language of worship

People express their deepest feelings about God in many ways. Music, art, mime, movement, words, paintings, statues, special clothing and holy words are all part of the special language of worship. Sometimes people gather together and find special comfort and strength from sharing the same beliefs and expressing them in the same way. Sometimes worship is a private act in which people prefer to be alone with their thoughts and prayers. The one thing all acts of worship have in common, however, is that they all help the worshipper to think about something or someone outside his or her ordinary world.

Religious pilgrimages

Religious worship is not confined to religious buildings. In many religions followers show their devotion to God by travelling to holy places and sites. This is called a pilgrimage. Making pilgrimages has been a popular way of expressing religious devotion since the fourth century, and it still is. Millions of people still travel to Canterbury, Walsingham, Rome, Jerusalem, **Makkah** and Benares, among other holy places. You can find out more about this aspect of religious worship in Unit 6.

In this unit

In this unit you will read about the following:

- The wide variety of worship found in different parts of the Christian Church. For most Churches, however, the most important act of worship is the service of **Holy Communion**. This is one of several **sacraments** celebrated in many churches.

- Jewish worship centres mainly around prayer. In Jewish life the home and the family are as important as the synagogue for worship.

- For Muslims worship also centres around prayer but this must be preceded by a washing ritual to make sure that the person is physically and mentally prepared before entering God's presence.

- Although many Hindus come to the mandir for worship, others worship God at home.

- For Sikhs time spent in the gurdwara for worship is important because they are in the company of the Guru Granth Sahib, the holy book. This book symbolises the presence of God.

- Buddhists visit their temple to pay their respects to and to show their love of the Buddha. While there, they spend time meditating on his teachings.

In the glossary

Divine Liturgy	Mandir
Holy Communion	Sacraments
Makkah	Temple

Jesus on worship

All the world's great religious leaders have stressed the importance of worship in developing the spiritual life. Jesus spoke for others when he said:

The hour comes, and now is here, when the true worshippers shall worship the Father in spirit and in truth; for the Father seeks such to worship him.

3 Religious worship

Christian worship

The need to worship God with other believers is felt by all Christians, although the form that this worship takes varies from Church to Church.

Anglican and Roman Catholic worship

The older Christian denominations, such as the Anglicans and Roman Catholics, usually follow a service taken from their own prayer book. In the Anglican Church there are two prayer books in common use. One, the *Book of Common Prayer*, dates back to the sixteenth century and uses language which is similar to the *Authorised Version* of the Bible. The other book, *Common Worship*, was brought into use in 2001. The Roman Catholic prayer book is called the Missal. Many people feel comfortable with services based on a prayer book because they have become familiar with the words it contains. In these churches the service of Holy Communion is far more important than any other. In Anglican churches it is held at least once a week but in Roman Catholic churches this service, called the **Mass**, is celebrated every day. The most important responsibility of the priest is to conduct the Mass.

Nonconformist worship

Nonconformist Churches do not use a prayer book. They believe that each act of worship should be inspired by the Holy Spirit. In Baptist and Methodist services the emphasis is very much on hymn singing, prayers that do not use a set form of words, readings from the Bible and a sermon. In a Salvation Army citadel the singing is usually led by a brass band but in many other churches a music group accompanies the music.

Some smaller churches do not have a priest or minister of their own to lead the worship. Usually members of the congregation take the service. Quakers rely on someone in the congregation being inspired to take the lead. Almost all their time spent together is taken up with silent prayer and reflection.

A Singing hymns and psalms is an important part of many church services

B There are some services, such as Holy Communion, which only a priest can conduct

Religious worship 3

C Most Christians feel it is important for them to meet together with other Christians to worship God

House churches
Although most worship still takes place in a **cathedral**, church or **chapel**, it has become popular in recent years for people to worship in house churches. As their name suggests, these are churches that began with people meeting in each other's houses. Some groups, however, have grown too big and have moved into larger premises. In recent years large Christian festivals, such as Spring Harvest and Greenbelt, have brought young Christians together to worship. Usually lasting for a week or two, these festivals not only give Christians the opportunity to worship together but also to spend time learning more about their faith.

In the glossary
Cathedral   Mass
Chapel

Find the answers
- What is the most important service in Anglican and Roman Catholic churches?
- What are you likely to find in most church services?
- In which Church is worship likely to be led by a brass band?

Learning about, learning from
1. Why do you think some Christians have chosen to worship in their friends' houses rather than in a church?
2. In pairs, write down four questions you would like to ask a Christian to find out more about worship in their church.
3. a. Describe something that makes Nonconformist worship different from Anglican or Roman Catholic worship.
   b. Why do Nonconformists choose to worship in this way?

Extra activity
Christians believe the whole of their lives should be 'an act of worship'. What do they mean by this?

3 Religious worship

The sacraments

The word sacrament comes from a Latin word meaning 'to make holy'. In most Churches it is the name given to the most important services. Christians in these Churches believe the sacraments are the most important way for them to receive God's blessings. In each sacrament something that can be seen, such as bread or water, is used to bring a spiritual blessing to worshippers.

Roman Catholic and Orthodox Churches

In Roman Catholic and Orthodox Churches there are seven sacraments:

- Baptism. During baptism water is poured on a person or they are immersed in it. The water is a symbol for the washing away of their sins. These two Churches baptise babies.
- **Confirmation**. During this service a person confirms the promises their parents and godparents made for them when they were baptised. In the Orthodox Church baptism and confirmation take place in the same service – **chrismation** – when the baby is a few weeks old. In the Catholic Church confirmation does not take place until the child is about nine years old.

- **Confession**. Many Christians confess their sins to a priest. They must show the priest that they are truly sorry (repentant) for their sins. In return, the priest pronounces **absolution** – God's forgiveness.
- **Ordination**. Ordination is the service in which a man becomes a priest. Both the Roman Catholic and Orthodox Churches consider ordination to be a sacrament and they ordain only men. In the ordination service a bishop lays his hands on the head of the person being ordained. This shows that the person has received God's blessing and the authority for the work he is going to do.
- Marriage. In the Orthodox and Roman Catholic Churches marriage is a sacrament by which God blesses two people who have become husband and wife. In a Roman Catholic service rings are given or exchanged as a symbol of God's blessing, while at an Orthodox wedding the man and the woman wear crowns. Other churches also marry people, of course, but they do not consider it to be a sacrament.
- Anointing the sick. When a person is old, seriously ill or dying the priest can anoint them with oil. This does not necessarily mean they are going to get better. It may prepare them for the journey they have to take through death.
- The **Eucharist**. This is the most important sacrament and is explained on pages 48 and 49.

Protestant and Nonconformist Churches

Most Protestants believe in only two sacraments – baptism and the Eucharist – because these two alone occur in the Gospels. Protestants believe God is always present when Christians worship together. Two Christian Churches, the Salvation

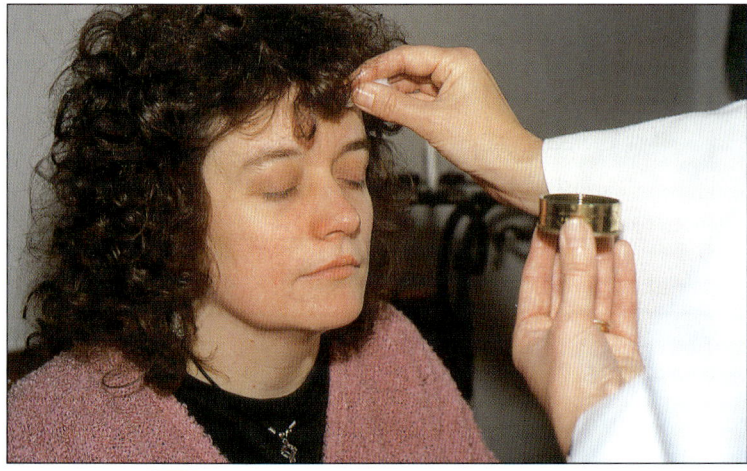

A This woman is being anointed with oil

Religious worship 3

Army and the Quakers, do not celebrate any of the sacraments. They believe that the whole of life is a sacrament.

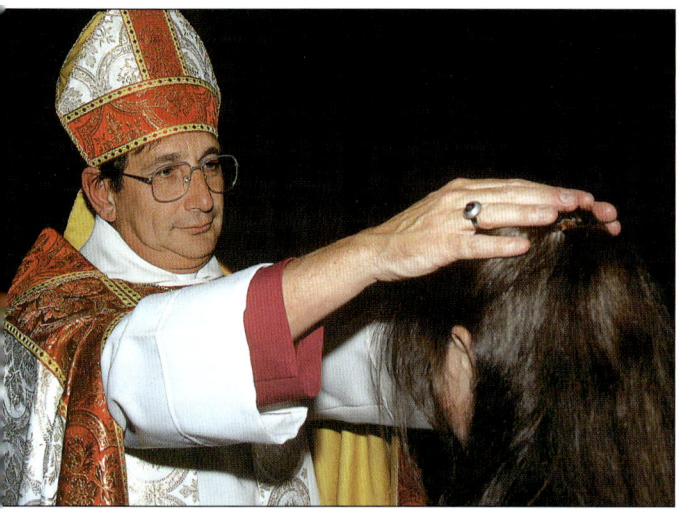

B Confirmation is a sacrament that gives a person the opportunity to make their own commitment to God

C The confession of sins to God through a priest is an important part of Catholic worship

In the glossary

Absolution　　　Confirmation
Chrismation　　Eucharist
Confession　　　Ordination

Find the answers

- What does the word 'sacrament' mean?
- What is the service of chrismation?
- What is absolution?

Learning about, learning from

1. **a.** How many sacraments are recognised by the Roman Catholic and Orthodox Churches?
   b. How many sacraments are recognised by the Protestant Church?
   c. How many sacraments are recognised by the Salvation Army and the Quakers?

2. **a.** List the seven sacraments celebrated by Roman Catholic and Orthodox Christians.
   b. Write one sentence about each sacrament. Leave a blank for the Eucharist and fill it in when you have read pages 48 and 49.

3. **a.** Are there moments in your life that you would call 'special' or 'holy'? What kind of moments would you give this description to?
   b. What do you think the Salvation Army and the Quakers mean when they call the whole of life a sacrament?

Extra activity

In a sacrament there is a physical symbol, for example water and bread, which bring a spiritual blessing. Why do you think physical symbols are needed?

47

3 Religious worship

Holy Communion

A The bread and wine on the table for Holy Communion remind all Christians of the body and blood of Jesus

The most important service for most Christians is the special meal at which they celebrate their belief that Jesus died and rose again to forgive their sins. At the service of Holy Communion worshippers share bread and wine, just as Jesus taught his disciples to do during the last meal he shared with them. This meal, the Last Supper, was described by Paul in one of his letters (see the box on the next page). It took place just a few hours before Jesus was put to death. The bread eaten during Holy Communion symbolises the crucified body of Jesus and the wine is a reminder of his blood.

One service, different names

The main Christian Churches have their own names and meanings for the service of Holy Communion:

- Roman Catholics call the service the Mass. They strongly believe that the bread and wine become the body and blood of Jesus during the service. The death of Jesus by which all sins are forgiven by God takes place each time the Mass is celebrated. The service is so important to Catholics that it is celebrated every day.
- In the Orthodox Church the service is called the Divine Liturgy. The 'liturgy' is an order of service that dates back to the earliest years of the Christian Church. Orthodox Christians trace the Divine Liturgy back to the early years of Christianity and this makes it special.
- Anglicans call their service the Eucharist ('thanksgiving') or Holy Communion. Some Anglicans, known as 'High Anglicans', share the Roman Catholic view of what happens to the bread and wine during the service. Others, called 'Evangelicals', hold a similar view to that of the Nonconformist Churches – they believe that the bread and wine are symbols of Christ's death and resurrection. As in the Roman Catholic Church, only ordained priests are allowed to conduct the service of Holy Communion in an Anglican church.
- Nonconformist Churches prefer to call their celebration of the death and

B The wine is handed over during the service of Holy Communion

resurrection of Jesus the **Lord's Supper** or **Breaking of Bread**. Nonconformists believe the bread and wine are symbols and no more. As with all Christian symbols, they are designed to help people to worship God but are not part of God or holy in themselves. The bread and wine simply help them to 'remember' the death of Jesus and to reflect on it.

Jesus's last meal

Paul describes why Christians celebrate Holy Communion:
For I received from the Lord what I also passed on to you: The Lord Jesus, on the night he was betrayed, took bread, and when he had given thanks, he broke it and said, 'This is my body, which is for you; do this in remembrance of me.' In the same way, after supper he took the cup, saying, 'This cup is the new covenant [agreement] in my blood; do this, whenever you drink it, in remembrance of me.'

Find the answers

- Which event do Christians remember and celebrate when they meet for Holy Communion?
- Whose example are Christians following when they hold the service of Holy Communion?
- Which Church often calls the service of Holy Communion the Eucharist and what does this word mean?

Religious worship 3

In the glossary
Breaking of Bread   Lord's Supper

Learning about, learning from

1. **a.** Draw the two symbols you can see in picture A.
   b. Why are these two symbols used in the service of Holy Communion?

2. Holy Communion is a 'holy meal'.
   a. What kind of occasion might bring people together to eat?
   b. How might people make a special effort to share food with others?
   c. Describe a meal you have shared that you can remember. What made the meal special?
   d. What makes Holy Communion a special service for most Christians?

3. **a.** List the different names and meanings that the various Churches give to the service of Holy Communion.
   b. From what you know about the different Christian Churches, explain how these acts of worship reflect the beliefs of each Church.

Extra activity

Most Christians agree that the service of Holy Communion is their most important act of worship. Why do you think they disagree over the meaning of the service?

3 Religious worship

Church leaders

There are some Churches that do not have ministers or priests. Instead they appoint their leaders from among the members of the congregation. This allows everyone to use their own gifts in the service of God. Even the Churches that do have priests call upon the services of members of their congregation, but some services in these Churches – such as the Eucharist – can be taken only by priests or ministers. This happens in the Anglican, Roman Catholic and Methodist Churches, among others.

Priests and bishops

After several years of training a person is ordained as a priest. There are no women priests in either the Roman Catholic or Orthodox Churches. These Churches believe that a priest has to be male because Jesus did not choose any women among his 12 disciples. Women, however, are allowed to be ministers in Nonconformist Churches and to be priests in the Church of England. They were first ordained in the Church of England in 1994, after a long debate lasting many years. In some parts of the Anglican Church there are now female bishops but not yet in the Church of England, which is a part of the Anglican Church.

The Pope is the leader of the Roman Catholic Church. He is also known as the Bishop of Rome. Senior bishops in the Roman Catholic Church are called **cardinals**. In both Roman Catholic and Anglican Churches bishops are senior priests who are responsible for looking after all the churches in an area known as a diocese. In the Anglican Church there are also **archbishops** who carry responsibility for the churches in a large area. The leader of the Anglican Church is the Archbishop of Canterbury.

Some services are taken only by a bishop. Bishops carry out most, but not all, confirmation services and all ordination services. Both these services involve the 'laying on of hands' on a person's head, a customary way of passing on a spiritual blessing.

In the Church of England priests carry out their work in local areas known as parishes. Everyone in England is in a parish and has a parish church, whether they are Christian or not. This is the church where many of them marry, have their children baptised and are buried. Usually today priests have more than one church to look after.

Priests are often helped in their work by lay workers who have been given the authority to carry out most services except Holy Communion. The Roman

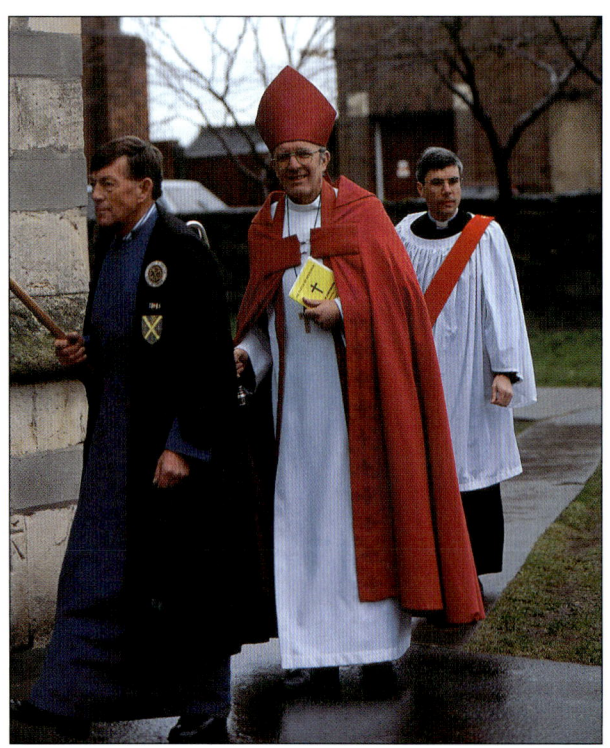

A Bishops are senior priests in the Anglican and Roman Catholic Churches and are given the responsibility of taking confirmation and ordination services

Religious worship 3

Catholic Church demands that its priests should not marry or have any sexual relations (**celibacy**).

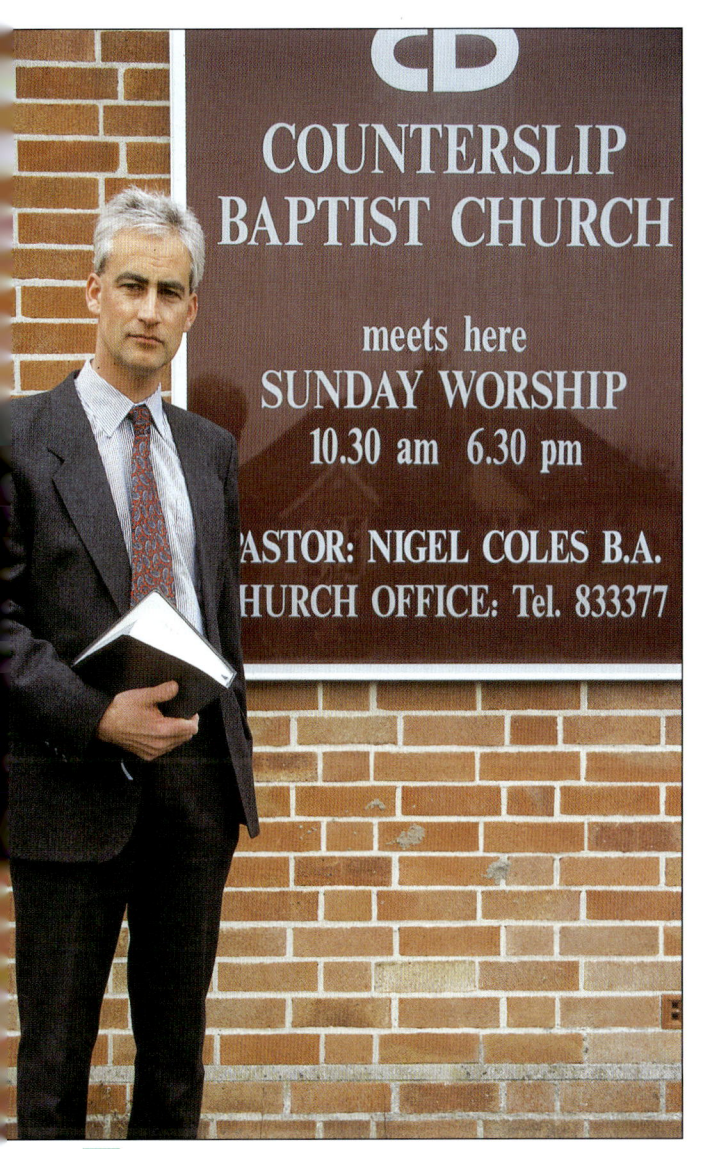

B The minister of a Baptist church

In the glossary
Archbishops   Celibacy
Cardinals

Learning about, learning from

1. The head of your school is the head teacher. He or she makes important decisions about how the school is run, helped by other people such as the deputy head.
   a. Do you play any part in the decision-making process?
   b. Do you think you should have more say in the way your school is run?
   c. Is it better to have specially trained people making the important decisions?

2. a. Which Churches allow women priests?
   b. What is the reason why some Churches do not allow women priests?
   c. Why do you think it took so long for female priests to be allowed in the Church of England?

Find the answers
- Who is the head of the Roman Catholic Church?
- Who leads the Anglican Church?
- Which service are people who are not ordained not allowed to take?

Extra activity

Roman Catholics believe that the Pope is linked back, through all the popes in history, to Jesus's disciple, Peter, the first Bishop of Rome. Using books from the library and/or the internet, find out how a new pope is chosen and discover what his responsibilities are as head of the Roman Catholic Church.

3 Religious worship

Jewish worship

The Jewish Sabbath Day begins at sunset on Friday evening and continues to nightfall on Saturday. During this time Jews are not allowed to do any work. Instead they enjoy the day of rest that God has given them. As the Talmud – a Jewish holy book – says, the Sabbath Day is one of God's greatest gifts to the Jews:

> God said to Moses, 'I have a precious gift in my treasure house. "Sabbath" is its name. Go and tell the people of Israel that I wish to give it to them.'

Sabbath worship

The Sabbath Day starts with the mother in a Jewish home lighting the special Sabbath candles. There are always two of them. One is to encourage everyone to 'observe' the Sabbath Day and the other is to tell them to 'remember' that, after creating the universe, God rested on the seventh day. They, too, must rest from all work on this day. The family then eat a special meal together.

On the Sabbath morning Jews go to the synagogue, many of them walking rather than using cars or public transport. The service can only begin when ten or more males, called a 'minyan', are present. In these synagogues men and women sit apart, with young children sitting with their mothers in the balcony.

Each person follows the service in their prayer book. One of the most important parts of the service is when the doors of the Ark are opened and the scroll of the Torah is taken out to be read from the bimah. It is a great honour to be asked to read from the scroll. In most synagogues this honour is given only to men, although in some synagogues women can also be invited to take the reading. The cover, crown and breastplate are then replaced on the scroll before it is returned to the Ark. During the service psalms are sung by the congregation. No musical instruments can be played on the Sabbath because that would involve work. Instead, in larger synagogues, the singing is led by the cantor, the song-leader.

Prayers form an important part of every Jewish act of worship. Many are recited or sung during Sabbath worship and this includes the **Shema**. The Shema, taken from Deuteronomy 6.4–9, is the most important statement of Jewish belief:

> Hear, O Israel! The Lord our God, the Lord is one! Love the Lord your God with all your heart and with all your soul and with all your strength.

The Shema reinforces the most important Jewish belief – that there is one God and that all other gods are false.

The Havdalah

The Sabbath Day ends with a simple but important ceremony, the **Havdalah**. The word means 'separation' – the service 'separates' the Sabbath from the week ahead. In the ceremony the father pronounces a blessing over his family. A

A Although most religious Jews attend worship in their local synagogue, the main worship activities centre around the home

Religious worship 3

special plaited candle is lit and a box containing spices, such as cloves, nutmeg and cinnamon, is passed around so that everyone can enjoy its fragrance. Everyone hopes that the week ahead will be similarly sweet smelling. The candle is put out in a glass of wine and the Sabbath ends as soon as three stars can be seen in the sky.

B Although women can conduct services in some synagogues, most rabbis are male

C In Jewish homes the Havdalah ceremony separates the Sabbath Day from the other days of the week

In the glossary
Havdalah   Shema

Find the answers
- What is one of God's greatest gifts to the Jewish people?
- On which day of the week do Jews remember God resting after spending six days creating the universe?
- What is a minyan?

Learning about, learning from

1. a. What is the Havdalah ceremony?
   b. What does the word 'Havdalah' mean?
   c. Why do people smell spices at Havdalah?

2. The Jewish people gave the world the idea of resting one day a week.
   a. Do you think we should be grateful for their gift? Explain your answer.
   b. Why do you think the Talmud describes the gift of a day's rest a week as a 'precious gift'?
   c. How do you think people might be encouraged today to treat one day a week as different from the others?

Extra activity

The Sabbath Day is welcomed into every Jewish home like an 'important visitor'. This tells us something very important about the Sabbath Day. Explain what you think this is.

3 Religious worship

Muslim worship

In some Muslim countries the **mu'adhin** climbs to the top of the **minaret** five times a day to issue the call to prayer. In other Muslim countries the call is played over loudspeakers. In Britain the same call goes out but it is more likely to be heard inside the mosque. Whichever method is used the words are always the same (see the translation in the box on the next page).

Washing

All male Muslims should attend the mosque for Friday midday prayers unless they are ill or travelling in a country which does not have a mosque nearby. On entering the mosque the shoes are removed as a sign of respect for Allah. Washing facilities are provided so that a washing ritual called **wudu** can be followed. The worshippers wash their hands, rinse their mouth and nostrils, wash their arms to the elbows, lightly wipe their forehead, ears and neck before washing both legs to the ankles. This is done three times and it is very important. It guarantees that the worshipper is both physically and spiritually clean before entering the presence of Allah.

A Muslim worship is an act of prayer to Allah

Friday prayers

Once the washing is over, the worshipper can enter the prayer hall of the mosque to pray to Allah. The Prophet Muhammad described prayer as 'a stream into which the faithful worshipper dives five times a day'.

Just as water cleanses the outside of a person's body, so prayer cleanses the soul. The prayers in the mosque are led by the **imam**, who takes all the worshippers through a different number of **rak'ahs** depending on the time of day. During each rak'ah, among other actions, a worshipper places his face to the ground twice while kneeling to show that he submits himself totally to the will of Allah. The name of the faith, Islam, means 'submission to Allah'.

Praying in a clean place

To a Muslim, worship means prayer and submission. Although Muslims prefer to pray in a mosque – especially at midday on Fridays – it is not essential. They can pray to Allah anywhere provided they are kneeling in a clean place. To guarantee this, a prayer mat is used. The mat is often plainly coloured, with a pattern containing an arch. While praying, the arch is pointed towards the holy city of Makkah. All prayer, inside and outside the mosque, takes place facing this direction. For British Muslims this means they must face south-east during prayer.

Muslim women pray in the same way as men, although men and women do not pray together. Looking after her family is a woman's main task and prayer has to be fitted in around this. Women sometimes go to the mosque to pray but this is not important. They are much more likely to say their prayers at home.

Religious worship 3

B Although Muslims often pray with other believers, each worshipper comes into the presence of Allah on their own

The call to prayer

God is the greatest. God is the greatest. God is the greatest. God is the greatest. I bear witness that there is no God but Allah. I bear witness that there is no God but Allah. I bear witness that Muhammad is the messenger of Allah. I bear witness that Muhammad is the messenger of Allah. Come to prayer. Come to prayer. Come to security. Come to security. God is the greatest. God is the greatest. There is no God but Allah.

In the glossary
Imam
Minaret
Mu'adhin
Rak'ahs
Wudu

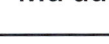

Find the answers
- What is the call to prayer?
- What is wudu?
- What is more important than prayer for women?

Learning about, learning from

1. Explain why you think Muslims do each of the following.
   a. Wash before they pray.
   b. Take off their shoes before they pray.
   c. Look straight ahead and not at other people as they pray.
   d. Stand shoulder-to-shoulder with other Muslims as they pray.

2. The Qur'an says: 'Prayer restrains from shameful and unjust deeds.' Why might prayer have this effect on people?

3. What do you think the Prophet Muhammad was teaching when he said: 'Prayer is a stream into which the faithful worshipper dives five times a day'?

Extra activity

The Prophet Muhammad said: 'Worship Allah as if you see Him; if you do not see Him know that He sees you.' What point is this making about Allah and prayer?

3 Religious worship

Hindu worship

The acts of worship carried out in the Hindu home are much more important than those performed in the mandir. The home is the centre of Hindu religious life. It is there that the traditions and beliefs of Hinduism are passed down from one generation to the next.

Worship in the home

Every religious Hindu has a shrine in his or her own home. This can be a separate room or simply a corner set aside for worship. It is here that an act of worship, a **puja**, is most likely to be carried out. There are no special days or times set aside for worship. Each family has its own personal god to whom the shrine is dedicated. Often this god is the much-loved Krishna, who was renowned for his love and kindness during the nine **avatars** (visits to earth) that Hindus believe he made to earth.

In the family it is the mother who makes sure offerings are made regularly to the family's god. She also ensures her children grow up knowing what is expected of them as Hindus. She organises the acts of puja early in the morning, at which the arti is lit. This is a lamp which has its wick dipped in ghee (clarified butter). At the same time, incense sticks are lit and the many names of God are repeated along with the daily prayer, the Gyatra Mantra (see the box on the next page). **Brahmins** (priests) repeat this prayer three times a day – at dawn, midday and sunset.

Worship in the mandir

Although most worship is offered at home, many Hindus also visit their local mandir regularly. They go along to offer devotion to God. They do this by lighting a candle, making an offering, saying their prayers, singing religious songs, and listening to some teaching from one of the priests. There is a path which makes its way around the mandir and people often walk along this as they say their prayers. Trees are holy in Hinduism and worshippers often visit them as part of their worship.

There is no set pattern of Hindu worship but everyone kneels in front of the shrine to offer their own puja. This usually involves making an offering of fruit or sweets. In return, the priest gives the worshipper a blessed offering of **prasad** (holy food), which has earlier been offered to the **murti**, the image of the god. A mark is made on the forehead of each worshipper with red powder. Everyone offers up their own prayers silently before the sweets presented as an offering are handed back to the worshipper. He or she eats a small part of the offering before giving what remains to everyone in the mandir, rich and poor.

A For Hindus, worship begins at home in front of the shrine

Religious worship 3

B Although a priest often leads the worship in the Hindu mandir, each worshipper makes their own offering and says their own prayers

The Gyatra Mantra

*Let us meditate on the glorious light of the creator,
May He guide our minds and inspire us with understanding.*

In the glossary

Avatars   Prasad
Brahmins   Puja
Murti

Find the answers

- Where does most Hindu worship take place?
- What is a puja?
- What might a person offer to the murti when they visit a mandir?

Learning about, learning from

1 Why is the home more important to Hindus than the mandir?

2 Describe two ways in which Hindus worship.

3 Imagine you are a Hindu who is looking for a special place to be set aside in your home for worship. Describe where you would choose and explain your answer.

4 Read the extract from the Gyatra Mantra in the box.
   a. What is meant by the phrase 'the glorious light of the creator'?
   b. How could meditation help and inspire people today?

Extra activity

Offering sacrifices and gifts to the gods is an important part of Hindu worship. These words of the god Krishna are found in the Bhagavad Gita: 'Whatever a zealous soul may offer, be it a leaf, fruit or water, that I willingly accept. For it was given in love.'
a. What do you notice about the three gifts which can be offered to Krishna?
b. What do you think it is that makes a gift acceptable to the god?

3 Religious worship

Sikh worship (1)

On entering a gurdwara each worshipper removes their shoes. They bow low in front of the Guru Granth Sahib and present their offerings of food and money. They then sit cross-legged on the carpeted floor, always below the level of the holy book. Sikhs say that sitting in front of the Guru Granth Sahib is just like being in the presence of God. As they take their place in the hall, worshippers are careful not to turn their back on the holy book at any time. To do so would show a lack of respect.

Sikh services

Anyone, male or female, can lead an act of worship in a gurdwara. However, it must be someone who is respected by other members of the congregation. The granthi, the only full-time official in the gurdwara, usually reads from the holy book and leads the prayers. He also waves a special fan called a **chauri** over the Guru Granth Sahib. This fan, traditionally made out of yak hair, is similar to the one that used to be waved over kings in India. By waving it over the holy book a similar degree of respect is shown.

Sikh men and women worship together but they do not sit together. Services are conducted in Punjabi, the language spoken by most Sikhs. Services may last for several hours and people are free to come and go as they please. However, everyone is expected to be in the gurdwara as the service draws to a close. As the aim of the service is mainly to give praise to God, much of it is taken up with singing hymns. These are taken from the Guru Granth Sahib and from other books containing the writings of the Gurus. The singing of hymns, which is called kirtan, is important for Sikhs. The music is led by a group of ragis (musicians) and the people do not always join in with it.

The Ardas and karah parshad

All services end with the Ardas prayer, which takes about 15 minutes to recite. This prayer, said by everyone standing and facing the Guru Granth Sahib, reminds people to remember God and the teachings of the ten Gurus. Prayers are also offered for Sikhs everywhere, particularly those in need.

While the Ardas is being recited, the karah parshad is stirred with a **kirpan**, a short sword. Karah parshad is holy food made from equal amounts of sugar, water, butter and semolina or plain flour. This is cooked in the gurdwara kitchen and brought in before the service ends. It is offered first to the Guru Granth Sahib and then to members of the congregation. Everyone stays for this special meal, bringing together all members of the Sikh community whether young or old, rich or poor, important or unimportant. The meal is also shared by visitors to the gurdwara, whether they are Sikhs or not.

A Holy food is shared among worshippers at the end of every Sikh act of worship

Religious worship 3

B The singing of hymns written by the Gurus is an important part of Sikh worship

The Ardas

Here is a short extract from the Ardas prayer:

O True King, O Loved Father, we have sung Thy sweet hymns, heard Thy life-giving Word... may these things find a loving place in our hearts and serve to draw our souls towards Thee. Save us, O Father, from lust, wrath, greed, undue attachment and pride... Give us light, give us understanding, so that we may know what pleases Thee. Forgive our sins.

In the glossary
Chauri Kirpan

Find the answers
- Who is the granthi?
- What is a chauri?
- Which important prayer is said during most Sikh services?

Learning about, learning from

1. Imagine you are interviewing a granthi from your local gurdwara for an article you are writing for the school magazine. List five questions you would like to ask him or her about worship in the gurdwara.

2. In the extract from the Ardas prayer in the box the worshipper asks God to save him from five things.
   a. Write a sentence about each of these things, showing that you understand what they mean.
   b. Where do you think a Sikh might go for 'light' and 'understanding'?

Extra activity

Sikhs say that being in front of the Guru Granth Sahib in the gurdwara is just like being in the presence of God. Explain what they mean by this.

59

3 Religious worship

Sikh worship (2)

Sikhs believe in **reincarnation**. This means that, when you die, your soul survives and moves on to live in another body. If a person has lived a good life in this life, they will move nearer to God in the next. If they have lived a bad life, they will be reborn in a worse state. The way to move closer to God is to follow the teachings of the Gurus. This is the only way to be freed from the cycle of birth and rebirth.

Sewa

All Sikhs try to serve others in this life, which is known as **sewa** ('service'). The whole point of sewa is to worship God through serving others. Sewa helps to purify the soul as well as acting as an example to other people.

There are many different ways in which Sikh worshippers try to live a life of sewa. For example, they may:

- serve others in the gurdwara by cleaning the building or working in the **langar** to prepare food for others
- spend time visiting the sick or the needy inside or outside the Sikh community
- work to raise money for charity
- give as much money as they can to help charitable causes. Guru Amar Das taught that all Sikhs should try to give 10 per cent of their income to those in need in the community. The Sikh leaders, however, recognise that this is not always possible. If some Sikhs have a lot of money it may mean more to them if they give their time instead of their money.

One principle of sewa is important. Help must be offered to anyone who needs it, no matter who they are or what their background is. Although talking about Sikhism is an important part of sewa, it should not be used to try to convert others to the faith. **Guru Nanak** spent a lot of time talking to Hindus and Muslims without trying to convince them that they were wrong.

Hiding good deeds

One group of Sikhs, the Namdhari Sikhs, teach that Guru Gobind Singh was not the last of the Sikhs Gurus. According to a later Guru, everyone should take every possible step to hide their good deeds from other people. The Namdhari Sikhs make their clothes from white cloth, which they spin at home to show the simplicity, purity and humility of the lives they lead.

A story

The following story is often told to illustrate the sewa that should characterise the lives of all true Sikhs. Guru Gobind Singh was leading his forces in a battle in which there were many casualties on both sides. The Guru's forces, after a bloody encounter, saw someone who was making his way among the injured, giving them water to drink. The man was a Sikh called

A The preparation of the food to be served in the langar involves many members of the Sikh community

Religious worship 3

Bhai Khanaya. They noticed he was giving water to everyone in need, whether Sikh or not.

The men complained to Guru Gobind Singh that Bhai Khanaya was helping the enemy and the Guru asked the man to appear before him. He did so and explained that many men were dying and the least he could do was to bring them some kind of comfort. The Guru announced that Bhai Khanaya was a good and faithful Sikh since all true believers must serve the needy, no matter who they are or what they believe.

B Serving food to others in the langar is an important act of love and charity for members of the gurdwara

From the Guru Granth Sahib

There is no worship without good deeds.

In the glossary
Guru Nanak
Langar
Reincarnation
Sewa

Find the answers
- What do Sikhs believe happens to a person's soul after death?
- How do Sikhs believe a person can move closer to God?
- How much of their income are Sikhs encouraged to give to the poor and needy?

Learning about, learning from

1. Write down five pieces of information about sewa, starting with an explanation of what it is.

2. Give three examples of what might be involved for someone putting sewa into practice.

3. Guru Nanak spent time talking to people who followed other religions, particularly Hindus and Muslims. He did not, however, try to convert them to his own religious faith. Do you think he set an example that others in the twenty-first century would do well to follow? Explain your answer.

Extra activity

Sikhs and Buddhists believe in a form of reincarnation, while Christians and Muslims believe in the resurrection of the body after death. Which of these two explanations are you more inclined to believe? Perhaps you have another explanation for life after death?

3 Religious worship

Buddhist worship

Both Hindus and Buddhists call their acts of worship puja. For Buddhists these acts of worship are carried out at a shrine. They may include chanting, making offerings before an image of the Buddha, listening to readings from the Buddhist holy books and reciting short passages together. Through their worship Buddhists are showing respect for the Buddha but they are not treating him as God. Worship provides the opportunity for them to be thankful for his teachings and to show their respect for him.

Acts of worship

Buddhists do not have to meet together or present gifts but most of them wish to do so. There are seven bowls of water on the shrine, which symbolise the things that a person would offer a guest in their own house. The Buddha is present at the shrine as an honoured visitor. There are flowers, candles and incense on the shrine to symbolise wisdom, death and kindness.

As Buddhists enter the shrine they put their hands together and bow in front of the statue of the Buddha. Sometimes they stand in front of the statue and touch their forehead, mouth and chest with their hands together. This shows that the mind, speech and heart are all involved when they offer their devotion.

People sit quietly to contemplate the image or to meditate. Some find it helpful to chant a simple **mantra**, which is like a prayer or blessing. These mantras are in the ancient language of Sanskrit and are repeated time and time again. Buddhists may use a mala – a string of prayer beads – to keep count of the number of times a mantra is chanted. The mantras might not have a straightforward meaning and it is their sound, rather than their meaning, which is important. You can read a mantra that a monk might use in the box on the next page.

The most well-known Buddhist mantra is 'Om mani padme hum', which means:

- om – a reminder of what Buddhists hope for in life
- mani – 'treasure', reminding worshippers of the Buddha, the Dhamma and the **Sangha**
- padme – meaning 'lotus'
- hum – reminding worshippers to be loving and kind.

In a Theravada shrine the image is always of the Buddha. In a Mahayana shrine, however, it can be of the Buddha or of a

A Meditation involves focusing your inner thoughts and is an important part of Buddhist worship

Religious worship 3

bodhissatva. A bodhissatva is a buddha who has reached enlightenment and now lives in a realm of the universe other than earth. He has delayed entering **nirvana** himself so that he can help and encourage others to reach enlightenment.

B Buddhist monks leave the temple after time spent meditating

A mantra

In reverence to the Buddha we offer incense
Incense whose fragrance fills the air
The fragrance of the perfect life, sweeter than incense
Spreads in all directions throughout the world.

In the glossary

Bodhissatva   Nirvana
Mantra   Sangha

Find the answers

- What is a puja?
- What is a Buddhist likely to lay before the image of the Buddha during an act of worship?
- Why might a Buddhist make use of prayer beads in their worship?

Learning about, learning from

1 Buddhists often touch their forehead, mouth and chest as they offer their devotion. What are they symbolising when they do this?

2 a. What do the seven bowls of water on the shrine represent?
  b. Why are flowers, incense and candles placed on the shrine?
  c. What is a mantra?
  d. What is a bodhissatva?

3 Read the words of the mantra in the box. What does this extract say about 'incense' and what does it say about the 'perfect life'?

Extra activity

Prayer wheels are important in Tibetan Buddhism. Turning them is a way of saying the mantras written on them, as it releases the words of the mantra into the world.

a. This suggests that suitable words can have a positive effect on the world. Do you think this is true?
b. Suggest two examples when words may have a positive effect.

4 Holy people

Introduction

Almost from the beginning of time there have been men and women noted for their dedication to God. In the Jewish faith, for example, there were prophets who were called by God to be His representatives to the people. The prophets were often reluctant to respond to God because they thought the people might not want to hear the message they were bringing. In a few cases their lives were put at risk by the work they had been given to do. At the same time, once God had chosen someone to be a prophet they could not avoid the calling.

Hindu holy people

The 'call of God' turned ordinary Jewish men and women into prophets. In Hinduism, however, holy men (**sadhus**) travel a different route. Living the life of a holy man is open to anyone in Hinduism once they reach the 'retirement' stage of life. By this time they have passed through the 'householder' phase and have carried out all their responsibilities to their family. They are now free to devote themselves to God and to wander from holy place to holy place. In India such holy men can often be found meditating beside rivers or on mountains – both holy natural symbols.

The Sikh Gurus

In Hinduism and Sikhism holy people are often called gurus or teachers. The first Guru in Sikhism was Guru Nanak, who gave the religion its shape and teachings. He was followed by nine other Gurus who each provided the growing faith with something distinctive and important, such as a collection of its holy books, the Sikh language, the holy city of **Amritsar** and the Golden Temple within that city. The last of the ten Gurus came and went but before he died he told people there would be no more human teachers. Instead, the people would be taught in future by the holy book, the Guru Granth Sahib, which would symbolise the presence of God in the Sikh community. God, through the holy book, became the teacher of the people and human teachers were no longer needed.

Other holy people

In the Christian faith over the last 2000 years many men and women have impressed others by their dedication to God. They have given themselves to lives spent in prayer and the service of others. During their lifetime they have usually gone about their work quietly, although some have lost their lives because of their Christian faith. It was often only after death that they were recognised as being particularly holy. The Roman Catholic Church recognises this and makes them saints although this takes place many years, perhaps centuries, after they have died.

In Christianity and Buddhism there have been a sizeable number of men and women down the centuries who have wanted to dedicate themselves to the spiritual life. They have become monks and nuns. In the case of Buddhism they can do this for a period of time before returning to normal life. In the case of Christianity, however, such a commitment is intended to be lifelong and rules out marriage. Christian nuns speak of being 'married' to God.

In this unit

In this unit you will read about the following:

- Christian saints such as Peter, Paul and the **Virgin Mary**, who are honoured for the holiness of their lives. Christian monks and nuns are men and women who have dedicated their lives to the service of God.

- The Jewish prophets who passed on to the people the message of God. Many of their writings are preserved in the Jewish scriptures.

- The imam in the Muslim community, who is important as the person who leads the prayers of the male believers in the mosque.

- Hindu holy men, or sadhus, who use the final part of their lives to wander in search of spiritual truth.

- The ten Sikh Gurus who laid the foundations of Sikhism through the example of their life and teachings.

- Buddhist monks who follow the example of the Buddha in devoting their lives to the search for enlightenment.

In the glossary

Amritsar
Golden Temple
Sadhus
Virgin Mary

From the Qur'an

God raised up prophets as bringers of good tidings and warners, and with them he sent down the Book with the truth to judge among the people regarding that in which they had differed.

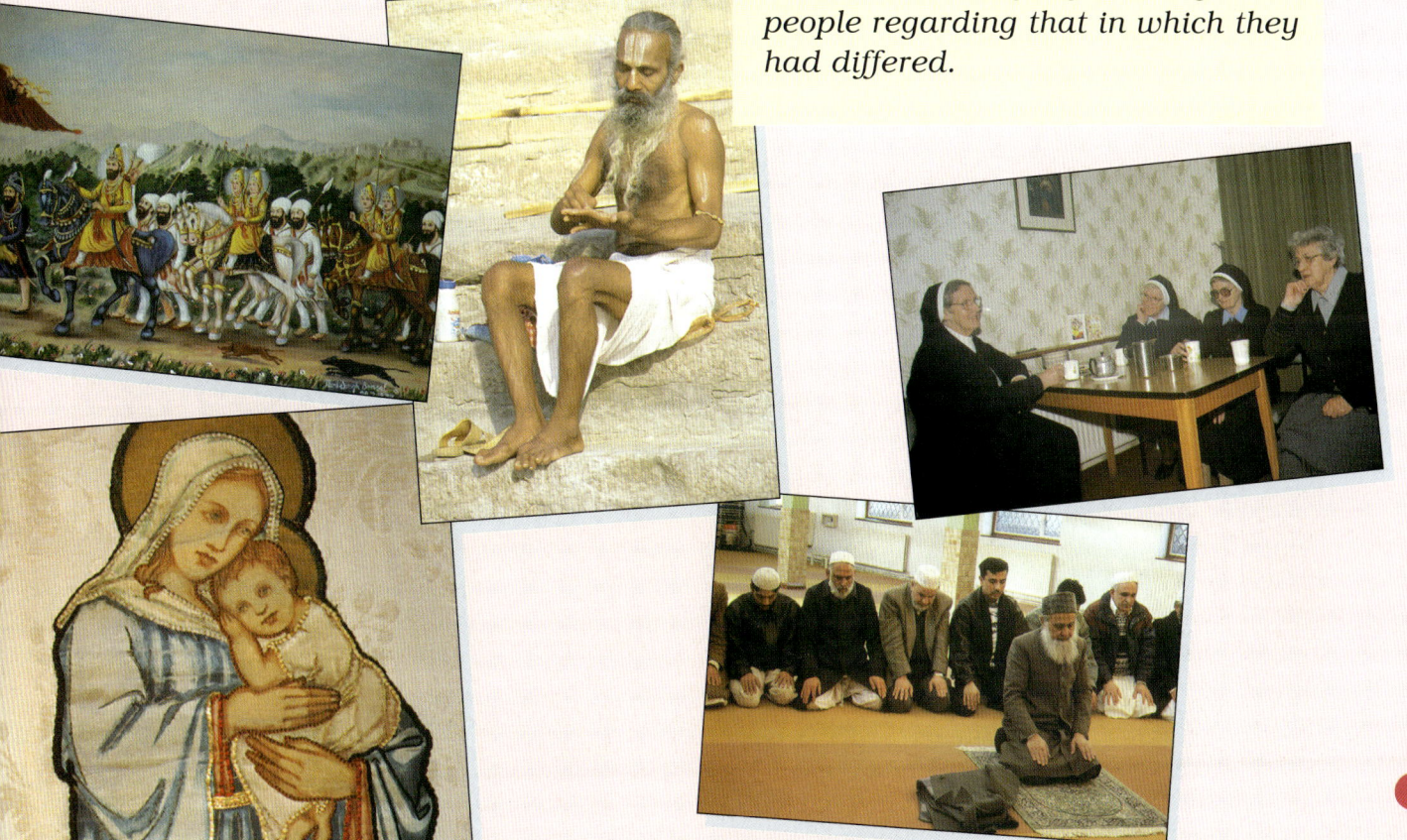

65

4 Holy people

Christian saints

A saint is a person in the Christian religion who has shown outstanding love and commitment to God throughout their lifetime. Often, though not always, a saint is also a martyr – someone who has lost their life because of their faith. Miracles are usually associated with the place where the saint was born, worked or died.

Early saints

The first recorded Christian saint and martyr was Stephen, whose death by stoning soon after the death of Jesus is recorded in the Acts of the Apostles in the New Testament. Some years later, both Peter and Paul met violent deaths at the hands of the Roman authorities. Although little is known for certain of the circumstances of their deaths, it is thought that they were killed by the Emperor Nero in around 64 CE. In the years that followed, most of the original 12 disciples of Jesus, now called 'apostles', were put to death.

In 155 CE the Christian leader, Polycarp, was slaughtered. After his death his bones were collected together by his followers. They were buried in a safe place but were dug up again when his followers met to commemorate his death. The day on which a martyr died was considered to be important. It was looked upon as the person's birthday in heaven – the day on which they were reunited with Christ.

Relics

It soon became the custom to bury the bones of a saint under the **altar** in a church. This was thought to be the most appropriate place for them to rest until Christ returns to earth. The bones, or **relics**, of a saint were also thought to be have special healing powers. This meant that the place where the bones were buried became a shrine – a place of pilgrimage for those seeking healing and help.

A The bones of saints have always been highly valued by some Christians

Holy people 4

B Many Christians believe the Virgin Mary is close to God in heaven and can help them with their prayers

Thousands of pilgrims travelled from shrine to shrine hoping to be cured. Relics were also believed to protect the church that housed them. In the Middle Ages churches often competed against each other to house the most valuable relics. Nowadays many of the most popular saints from the past have been largely forgotten. Others, however, still live on in the names of Roman Catholic and Anglican churches.

Making saints

Saints are 'made' by the Roman Catholic Church. Often this might not be until centuries have passed since the person's death. A close examination of the person's life is carried out before they are declared to be a saint. There must also be at least two miracles associated with them before they can become a saint. The present Pope in Rome, Jean Paul II, has made more people saints than any other pope in history. One or two of them, such as Mother Theresa of Calcutta, died only towards the end of the twentieth century.

In the glossary
Altar   Relics

St Polycarp

The Romans told Polycarp that he did not have to die: if he gave up his Christian faith they would release him. He is said to have replied:
For 86 years I have been Christ's servant and he has never done me wrong; how can I blaspheme my king who saved me?

Find the answers
- What is a saint?
- What is a martyr?
- What is a relic?

Learning about, learning from
1. a. How would you recognise a saint if you saw one?
   b. What makes a person a saint?
   c. Which people from the modern world would you make saints if you were the Pope?

2. a. Why have saintly people in the past often been persecuted and put to death?
   b. What might be the value to Christians of keeping the bones of a saint?
   c. Can you identify any dangers in keeping relics?

Extra activity
Read the quotation by St Polycarp in the box. What do you think Polycarp meant when he said these words?

4 Holy people

Christian monks and nuns

A Monks and nuns believe that they need to be poor to be able to work among the poorer members of society

Monks and nuns are men and women who have chosen to devote their whole life to serving God. They are particularly important in the history and traditions of two religions, Christianity and Buddhism.

Early Christian monks
Soon after the Christian Church began, many men and women wanted to cut themselves off from the outside world and give themselves totally to God. Like Jesus before them, they went into the desert to pray. Many monks and hermits (people who live totally alone) went to Mount Athos in Greece and, before long, a number of monasteries had been built in the area. About 20 monasteries remain there to this day, housing thousands of Orthodox monks.

The vows
St Benedict (480–547 CE), who founded the Benedictine order of monks, laid down a set of rules for those who wanted to join the community. They became known as 'the Rule' and they were soon adopted by other monastic communities. Each monk and nun had to keep three promises or vows:

- The vow to live in total poverty with no earthly possessions or comforts. Anything a person brings with them when they join becomes the property of the monastery or convent.
- The vow to abstain from all sexual relationships (celibacy). For nuns this takes the form of being 'married' to God. The wearing of a wedding ring is a symbol of this marriage.
- The vow to live in total obedience to the will of the community. In a convent this will is expressed by the Mother Superior and in a monastery by the abbot. The leaders are usually chosen by the monks and nuns themselves for the holiness of their lives.

Living the holy life
Ever since the first monasteries and convents were built the most important

Holy people 4

emphasis has been placed on following a life of prayer. Traditionally there are seven services, largely of prayer, during a monastic day, starting with Lauds in the very early morning and running through to Compline in the late evening. In most modern communities, however, this number has been reduced to four.

Although a few 'closed' communities remain, which have little contact with the outside world, this is not true of most monasteries and convents. In most communities some members work inside on such things as gardening or making things to sell, while others leave each day to work in jobs such as teaching or nursing. Convents are often attached to local Roman Catholic churches to help the priest in his work.

B Although the monastic life is one of prayer, most people in a monastery or convent work in the outside world as well

Find the answers
- What is a monk?
- What is a nun?
- What is a hermit?

Learning about, learning from

1. **a.** Which three vows are taken by a monk and a nun when they join a monastic community?
   b. Why were these three promises chosen to be required of all members of a monastery or convent?
   c. The rules of a convent or monastery are strict. Would you describe the rules of your school as strict? Do you think rules are a good thing or a bad thing?

2. Fewer people are becoming monks and nuns each year.
   a. What makes a person decide to become a monk or a nun?
   b. What effects would it have on you, good and bad, if you were to join a monastic order?

Extra activity

Imagine you have been put in charge of a programme to attract more young people into becoming monks and nuns.
a. What kind of things would you do and say?
b. How could you make the monastic way of life as attractive as possible to young people today?

4 Holy people

Jewish prophets

In early Jewish history a prophet was a man or woman sent to deliver God's message to the people. Sometimes the prophet would look into the future and talk about events that had not yet happened. More usually, however, he or she passed judgement on the way the people were living at the present time. The first, and the greatest, of the Jewish prophets was Moses.

The prophets

The later prophets were to play an important part in Jewish history. Among them were Amos, a herdsman, who suddenly appeared in the marketplace and started to preach the judgement of God to the people. Another prophet, Hosea, used his own life story to illustrate how loving and forgiving God is. His wife had been unfaithful to him and he told the Israelites that they, too, had been unfaithful to God by worshipping other gods. In the eyes of all Jewish prophets the worship of idols (idolatry) was the worst sin the people could commit. However, just as Hosea had taken back his unfaithful wife, God would always welcome back those who were truly sorry – as long as they showed it by leading a very different life.

A long line of prophets followed, who told people that God would surely judge and punish them. Isaiah said that God was holy while the nation of Israel was full of hypocrites. The prophets hated those people who said one thing and did another. There were too many people who kept all the religious laws and yet did not look after the poor and helpless around them. As you may imagine, this message of the prophets was not popular with the people. One prophet, Jeremiah, upset so many people with his message that he was branded a traitor and thrown into prison. He told the people that unless they changed their ways they would be destroyed.

Jeremiah was not the last of the prophets to suffer. Daniel was thrown into a lion's den because he refused to stop praying to God when the king told him to do so. Like Jeremiah, though, Daniel survived because God was with him. So, too, did Jonah, who was swallowed by a great fish because he refused to preach God's word to the people of Nineveh.

The scriptures and the prophets

The Jewish scriptures are divided into three sections, of which one is the books of the prophets. After the five books of the Torah, those of the prophets are the most important. They are divided into two groups:

A Moses gave the Jewish people the Ten Commandments and is recognised as one of the most important leaders of Judaism

Holy people 4

- The major prophets, so called because they are much longer than the other books: Isaiah, Jeremiah and Ezekiel.
- The minor prophets: Daniel, Hosea, Joel, Amos, Obadiah, Jonah, Micah, Nahum, Habakkuk, Zephaniah, Haggai, Zechariah and Malachi.

In order that the lessons taught by the prophets are learned by Jews today, passages are read from the prophets after the Torah passage in the synagogue on the Sabbath Day and during most festival services.

B Jeremiah was a Jewish prophet who suffered a great deal because of his faith in God

Find the answers

- What is a prophet?
- Which prophet used the story of his own life to show how faithful and loving God was?
- Which prophet was thrown into prison because the people did not want to hear his message?

Learning about, learning from

1 Here is a crossword with the answers filled in. Copy it into your exercise book or file. Write down a one-sentence clue for each answer.

¹J	E	R	E	M	²I	A	H
					D		
					O		
					L		
			³M		A		
⁴P	R	O	P	H	E	T	
			S		R		
			E		Y		
⁵H	O	S	E	A			

2 Imagine if a prophet like one you have read about were to visit Britain today.
   a. What kinds of things would he or she be happy and unhappy about?
   b. What kind of reception might he be given? Would he be welcomed or not?

Extra activity

From the message preached by the prophets it seems that God was more concerned with the hypocrisy of the people than by the things they actually did.
a. Explain what hypocrisy is.
b. Why was God was so upset by hypocrisy?

4 Holy people

Muslim imams

The Arabic word 'imam' means 'to stand in the front' and this is a clue to the main function of the imam in a mosque. He is the man who stands in front of the lines of worshippers, leading them as they move through the rak'ahs and recite their set prayers.

The imam

The imam has no special training for his work and is not ordained as a holy man. There are no priests or monks in Islam. This is because each member of the Muslim community is believed to be equal in the sight of Allah. An imam is an educated person who is chosen by the Muslim community to lead their prayers because he is recognised by everyone as a good Muslim. In addition, he must:

- have a good understanding of the faith and its teachings
- have earned the respect of his fellow Muslims so that they will follow his leadership
- be known for his own holiness of life and that of his family
- have studied the Qur'an.

Friday prayers and other duties

Every Friday at noon Muslim men gather at their local mosque for prayers. This is the most important act of religious worship in the week. Before the service begins the imam usually acts as the khatib, the person who preaches the Friday sermon. In this he explains a passage from the Qur'an or a story about the Prophet Muhammad. The imam then leads the worshippers in several rak'ahs.

The imam is also expected to carry out other religious and social responsibilities. He teaches about Islam to people of all ages. Muslim children attend the madrasah – the school attached to the mosque – from the age of four onwards, where they learn to read and speak the Qur'an in Arabic. The imam sometimes performs religious ceremonies and services like weddings and funerals, although he does not have to be present at these services. People often go to the

A It is important that the imam of a mosque should have a good knowledge of the Qur'an

Holy people 4

imam to seek religious advice, especially when they are not sure of the teaching of the Qur'an on a particular topic. The imam might visit a local prison to provide instruction in the faith for Muslim inmates and also to help find a home and work for them when they leave. He is also likely to visit members of the community who are too old or too sick to attend services in the mosque.

In small mosques there is unlikely to be a full-time imam. Instead, someone may take on the responsibility voluntarily and have a regular job as well. As long as they understand the Qur'an, a person can lead prayers in a mosque without being an imam. In large mosques there may be several imams, each with their own areas of responsibility.

B The most important responsibility of the imam is to lead daily prayers in the mosque

Find the answers

- Why are there no priests in Islam?
- What is the most important religious occasion in the week in a mosque?
- Where do children learn about their faith and the Arabic language?

Learning about, learning from

1. **a.** What does the word 'imam' mean?
   b. Why is the name of the imam particularly appropriate?
   c. Why does the imam need to be an educated man?
   d. Why it is incorrect to speak of the imam as a priest?

2. **a.** Why is it important for the imam to be known for the holiness of his life?
   b. Why is it important for the imam's family also to be known for the holiness of their lives?

3. In your own words, describe three responsibilities of the imam of a mosque.

Extra activity

Although the imam may take certain services such as marriages and funerals, it is not necessary for him to do so. Other members of the community can take these services. What does this say about Islam?

4 Holy people

Hindu sadhus

For Hindus, life is rather like taking a journey. As we grow up we have many new experiences, visit new places, meet new people and learn new skills. We grow from childhood though to adulthood, then we might marry and have children, watching them grow up before we grow old and eventually die. At each stage in the life process we make decisions that may have serious consequences for our future. For Hindus, making the right decisions is all-important. It is important to make sure that no bad **karma** is collected along the way.

Hinduism teaches that each person passes through 16 **samskaras** on their journey from conception to death. A samskara is a ritual or ceremony which marks a new stage that has been reached in a person's life and helps them on their way.

Old age

Marriage is important because it marks the beginning of the 'householder' phase in a person's life. After marriage they spend most of the rest of their lives as householders. They go to work, have children and make a contribution to the community to which they belong. As they grow older and have less responsibility at home, however, some Hindu men play less of a part in everyday life and give more time to thinking about God and the next life. They may become a religious teacher, passing on their wisdom to others. This is the fourteenth samskara.

By this time a Hindu man's children will have grown up and married. He no longer carries a responsibility for them. They have left home and set up their own homes. He is free to retire and devote himself to a study of the Hindu scriptures and to prayer. To release him still further he might live with one of his sons. Sometimes, in India, he may even leave home and live in a forest, a particularly holy place in Hinduism. He may choose to go on a long pilgrimage. His wife may travel with him or she may prefer to stay at home.

Sometimes a Hindu man may give up (renounce) everything – including all his possessions and family – and travel for the rest of his life. A man who does this is called a sadhu – a saintly or holy person.

A Each religious Hindu man can spend his retirement searching for the meaning of life if he wishes

Holy people 4

A sadhu may spend the rest of his days wandering in the countryside, wearing just a loin-cloth around his waist and carrying no more than a food bowl and a water pot. He may choose to spend much of his time on the banks of the holy River Ganges.

Most sadhus are old but occasionally a Hindu may decide to become a wandering holy man while he is still young. This is a big decision for anyone to take because it means he will never be able to marry, have children, own any possessions of his own or go to work. Since a Hindu's children are his hope and security for the future, few men are prepared to make this sacrifice. The life of the sadhu is one of constantly moving around while thinking about the mysteries of birth, life, death and rebirth. By doing this he hopes that he might gain moksha – the final release from the cycle of birth, death and rebirth – but few people do achieve this. It is believed that most return in the next life to go through the cycle again.

B Hindu priests (brahmins) conduct worship in the local mandir

In the glossary
Karma   Samskaras

Find the answers
- What is karma?
- What is a samskara?
- What is a sadhu?

Learning about, learning from

1. a. What is the fourteenth samskara for a Hindu?
   b. When in life may a person decide to take this step?
   c. Why might he decide not to take this step?

2. Do you think it is easy to be a sadhu? Give as many reasons as you can for your answer.

3. a. Which stages have been the most important in your life and which stages are likely to be important in the future?
   b. Write down 12 important stages in life. Why are they so important?

Extra activity
Imagine you are a Hindu who is approaching the time when he could retire. Do you think you would consider becoming a wandering holy man? Which arguments would persuade you one way or the other?

4 Holy people

Sikh Gurus

A Guru Nanak (left), the first Sikh Guru

In India a Guru is a spiritual teacher. In Sikhism there have been ten human Gurus and they are all greatly respected. The first, and the founder of Sikhism, was Guru Nanak (1469–1539), who laid down the basic teachings of the faith. The last of them was Guru Gobind Singh (1666–1708), who told the people that God would not send them any more human spiritual teachers. Instead, they should from now on look to the holy book, the Guru Granth Sahib, to guide and teach them.

The Gurus

Guru Nanak died in 1539 and he chose one of his followers, Lehna (Guru Angad), to succeed him. Guru Angad made the Punjabi language known to the people so that they could sing the many hymns of Guru Nanak. When Guru Amar Das (1479–1574) became leader he insisted that every Sikh place of worship (gurdwara) should have a kitchen called a langar. There, rich and poor people could sit down together on equal terms and eat the same food. This has been a feature of every gurdwara built since then.

Guru Ram Das (1534–1581) founded the holy city of Amritsar in 1577. Amritsar has become a place of pilgrimage for all Sikhs. The next Guru, Guru Arjan (1563–1606), built the Golden Temple in Amritsar and compiled the holy book, the Guru Granth Sahib, for everyone to read. He also became the first Sikh martyr. Burning sand was poured over his body by Turks before he was made to sit in scalding water and roasted to death.

The sixth Guru, Guru Har Gobind (1595–1644), encouraged Sikhs to be prepared to die for their faith if necessary. Guru Har Rai (1630–1661) and Guru Har Krishan (1656–1664) were able to lead peaceful lives but the ninth Guru, Guru Tegh Bahadur (1621–1675) was beheaded by a Muslim emperor of India for insisting that all Sikhs had the right to worship God in their own way.

The Khalsa

During the time of Guru Gobind Singh, the tenth and last of the Gurus, Sikhs underwent severe persecution. In 1699 Guru Gobind Singh called them all together in Anandpur. With a drawn sword he asked the assembled Sikhs:

> Is there anyone who will give up his head to prove his faith in me?

One man volunteered and went into the tent with Guru Gobind Singh. There was a

Holy people 4

thud and blood poured out from under the tent. This happened four more times with other volunteers and then all five men came out of the tent together. This was Guru Gobind Singh's way of checking their commitment and they all passed the toughest possible test.

These five Sikhs became the first members of the **Khalsa** ('the pure ones'). They became known as the Panj Piares. Today, Sikhs – men and women – are challenged to be initiated into the Khalsa and so prove their commitment to God and the faith. The initiation is carried out by five respected Sikhs, representing the Panj Piares, in the gurdwara.

B Guru Gobind Singh, the last of the ten Sikh Gurus, leads the procession

The true Guru

Guru Nanak insisted that:
The true Guru is the one who eats what he earns through honest work, and gives from what he has to those in need – he alone knows the true way to live.

In the glossary
Khalsa

Find the answers
- What is a Guru?
- Who was the first Guru and what did he give to Sikhism?
- Who built the Golden Temple in Amritsar?

Learning about, learning from

1 a. Why are some people, like the Sikh Gurus, prepared to die for their religious faith?
  b. Is there anything you feel so strongly about that you might be prepared to die for it?

2 Guru Nanak taught that there were many false gurus. Read the extract about the true Guru in the box and describe, in your own words, what a true spiritual teacher would be like.

Extra activity

As well as calling their early leaders Gurus, Sikhs also give the same title to God.
a. What do they mean when they call God 'the true Guru'?
b. Write down two differences between God the Guru and the ten human Gurus.

4 Holy people

Buddhist monks and nuns

The teaching of the Buddha aims to help people on their spiritual journey to nirvana. The community of Buddhist monks has always been especially important in Theravada Buddhism because the simplicity of monastic life makes the pilgrimage towards nirvana easier.

Being a monk

Children can become novice monks from the age of seven. They will not be fully ordained as a monk, however, until they reach the age of 20. They can leave the monastery at any time. It is believed that sharing the monastic life is a great spiritual blessing to them even if they stay only for a short time. In some Buddhist traditions girls can also spend time in a monastery.

Monks get up before sunrise and meditate before sweeping the monastery and tending the garden. They set off in a line from the monastery to collect their food from local Buddhist householders. The monks do not need to beg because people want to give them alms (gifts). These gifts can be food or clothing, but not money. Buddhism teaches that it is far more important to give than to receive. It is not only a Buddhist's duty to give to the monks but to do so also helps them in their attempt to reach nirvana.

The monks eat their main course before noon and then fast until the next morning. They may drink water or tea while they fast as long as it does not contain milk or sugar. They study and pray, receive friends and are available to give people advice and help. The monks also go out to schools and colleges to give talks about Buddhism. They might visit those who are ill in hospital or in prison. In the early evening the monks often teach those people who come to the **vihara**. The last part of the day is devoted to study and meditation.

Living simply

Most Buddhist monks live on their own in a small hut in the monastery. Their rooms are very simple with perhaps just a bed, a small table and a chair. Most prefer to sit on the floor. Some rooms also have a small shrine. All that a monk possesses are:

- two robes and thread to repair them when they wear out
- a razor – most monks keep their heads shaved
- a bowl in which people place gifts
- a cup for food and drink
- a special strainer to remove any insects from the drinking water – the Buddha taught his followers that they must not kill any living thing, not even by accident.

A The life of a Buddhist monk is largely split between meditation, reading the scriptures and working

Holy people 4

All Buddhists are expected to keep the Five Precepts, which are a guide for everyday life. In addition, monks and nuns are expected to keep five extra rules. You can read these in the box below.

B Buddhists in the community provide the material from which a monk makes his own robes

The ten rules

The Five Precepts are:
- not to harm any living creature
- not to take anything from someone which has not been given by them
- not to take part in any improper sexual activity
- not to use any improper speech
- not to drink any alcohol or to misuse any drugs.

The additional rules for monks and nuns are:
- not to eat anything after midday
- not to listen to music or to dance
- not to use perfume or jewellery
- not to sleep on a soft bed
- not to accept gifts of money.

In the glossary
Vihara

Find the answers
- Who makes sure that the monks have food and clothes?
- What did the Buddha teach his followers about killing living things?
- Which set of rules act as a guide for all Buddhists?

Learning about, learning from
1. Monks have few possessions. Those they do have may include robes, a sun umbrella, some thread, a razor and an alms bowl. Write a sentence for each item, explaining why each of them is important.

2. a. What are alms?
   b. Why are alms important to Buddhist monks?
   c. Why are Buddhists pleased to give alms to monks?

3. If you were a Buddhist parent would you want your child to be educated for a short time by Buddhist monks? What do you think he might learn from them that he would not learn at an ordinary school?

Extra activity
a. Why do Buddhist monks rely on others to provide them with food?
b. What spiritual lesson do you think this dependency teaches them?

5 Religious symbols

Introduction

A symbol can be anything that stands for something else. Symbols are often used to represent things that are otherwise difficult to describe. Words do not seem enough when people try to describe God and what He is like. Many religious people believe that human beings can never really know God and so symbols are a good way for people to show what they believe about Him. Symbols are able to point the religious worshipper towards God.

Christian symbols

The usefulness of symbols in religious worship can be seen when we look at Christianity. Christians believe God to be an all-powerful, invisible and all-loving Spirit. As such, He is beyond all human experience. The gulf between God and humans can only be bridged if links are found. This is where symbols come in.

One useful link for Christians is to call God their 'Father'. The prayer that Jesus taught his disciples to use – the Lord's Prayer – begins with the words: 'Our Father who is in heaven'.

When Christians refer to God as 'their Father' they do not mean that God has 'fathered' them in the same way as their human father has done. What they are really saying is that God treats them in the same way as one would expect the perfect human father to treat his children. Such a person, of course, does not exist, but if he did he would act firmly with discipline and yet always with love and tenderness. The symbol – the fatherhood of God – points Christians towards truths about God. This is what every useful religious symbol sets out to do.

Other religious symbols

Every religion has its own distinctive symbols. They may take the form of objects that can be found in places of worship. In the Muslim mosque, for example, the **minbar** and the **mihrab** are important symbols, while in the Jewish synagogue the same can be said of the Ark. Clothes worn as a part of religious worship are also likely to have an important symbolic meaning. This is true of the **tallit** and **tefillin** worn by Jewish men during prayers and the **turban** worn by Sikh men. Religious practices can also be symbolic. The Muslim prayer ritual, the rak'ah, expresses the deepest feelings that believers hold about Allah. These feelings cannot be expressed in any other way.

Most religious buildings are full of symbols. Two examples are the crescent moon outside a mosque and the seven-branched candlestick (**menorah**) in a synagogue. The flag which flies over every Sikh gurdwara is also an important symbol.

Statues and likenesses of God are controversial symbols. The followers of some religions believe it is totally wrong to represent God with statues and pictures. For others, though, a statue helps to focus their hearts and minds on God. As Hindus point out, the murtis in their religion are no more than symbols of God. They do not believe they are really God and they do not worship them. They worship the reality, God, who is represented by the images.

In this unit

In this unit you will read about the following:

- The Christian symbols, the most important of which is the cross.
- The main Jewish symbols, ranging from those in the home, such as the **mezuzah**, to those in the synagogue, such as the Ark.
- Muslim symbols, especially those in the mosque. These include the minarets, which remind worshippers of the central beliefs of their faith.
- The main Hindu symbols, especially **Ganesha** and the sacred syllable.
- The Sikh symbols of the gurdwara and the **Five Ks**.
- The Buddhist symbols of the lotus flower, the eight-spoked wheel and the statue of the Buddha.

In the glossary

Five Ks	Minbar
Ganesha	Tallit
Menorah	Tefillin
Mezuzah	Turban
Mihrab	

From the scriptures

Muslims, Sikhs, Christians and Jews are forbidden to make any representation of God. These words are taken from the Jewish and Christian scriptures:

You shall not make for yourself an idol in the form of anything in heaven or on earth beneath or in the waters below. You shall not bow down to them or worship them; for I, the Lord your God, am a jealous God, punishing the children for the sins of the fathers to the third or fourth generations.

81

5 Religious symbols

Christian symbols

Christians have always found symbols particularly useful in their worship. Hiding from terrible persecution in the Roman Empire, for example, the early Christians drew symbols on the walls of the catacombs (vast tunnels beneath Rome). When other Christians saw the symbols they were encouraged by the knowledge that their friends were nearby. Their enemies, on the other hand, could not understand what the symbols meant.

One of the most popular symbols at the time was the fish. It was used because each letter of the Greek word for fish (icthus) stood for the phrase:

I – Jesus
C – Christ
TH – God
U – Son
S – Saviour

Many modern Christians have revived this symbol by sticking it on their cars or by wearing it as a lapel badge.

Symbols in worship

Christian worship is full of symbols and this is particularly true of the different sacraments. At the heart of the Eucharist are the symbols of bread and wine. In the service of baptism, water is used as a symbol of spiritual washing and cleansing. In most churches babies are baptised (**infant baptism**) but in the Baptist Church and a few others only adults pass through the waters (**believer's baptism**). When the bishop lays his hands on the heads of people during confirmation he is showing them that they have received the Holy Spirit, just as the first disciples did on the Day of Pentecost. This symbol of the 'laying on of hands' is used in more than one Christian ceremony.

At the serious, and yet joyful, season of Easter, symbols help worshippers to think deeply about the death and resurrection of Jesus. One of these symbols – the paschal candle – is lit in many churches between the festivals of Easter and Pentecost to symbolise Christians moving from darkness to light because of the resurrection of Jesus.

The cross as a symbol

The most important, and most powerful, Christian symbol is the cross. This symbol is found inside and outside most churches. It reminds people of the death of Jesus for the sins of the whole world. Sometimes there is the figure of Jesus on the cross and then it is called a **crucifix**. Christians often wear small crucifixes around their necks to show that they are members of the Church.

Some Christians, mostly Roman Catholic and Orthodox Christians, touch their forehead, chest and shoulders with their hand to make the 'sign of the cross' across their body during certain acts of worship. Some people also genuflect (kneel briefly on one knee) and make the sign of the cross as they pass in front of the altar in a church. At the end of a service the priest sometimes blesses the congregation by making the same sign over them.

A Candles are used in most churches to symbolise the light that Jesus brought into the world

Religious symbols 5

B The cross is a reminder of the death of Jesus

The witness of Avircius

The following inscription was found on the tombstone of an early Christian:

My name is Avircius, a disciple of the pure Shepherd, who feeds the flocks of sheep on the mountains and plains, who has great and all-seeing eyes. He taught me the faithful Scriptures. To Rome he sent me. Everywhere I met with brethren. With Paul before me, I followed, and Faith everywhere led the way and served food everywhere, the Fish from the spring – immense, pure, which the pure virgin caught and gave to her friends to eat for ever, with good wine, giving the cup with wine.

In the glossary

Believer's baptism   Infant baptism
Crucifix

Find the answers

- Which symbol gave Christians great courage when they were being persecuted by the Romans?
- In which Christian celebrations do symbols play an important part?
- What is the most important Christian symbol?

Learning about, learning from

1. Explain in a sentence the meaning of the following words or phrases.
   a. Baptism.
   b. Infant baptism.
   c. Believer's baptism.
   d. Bishop.
   e. Confirmation.
   f. Altar.

2. What is the difference between a cross and a crucifix?

3. Imagine you are a Christian living in Rome during the time of Roman persecution. Do you think you would have found it a great comfort to know that you could communicate with other Christians – if only by using symbols? What kind of comfort might it have given you?

Extra activity

Water is an important Christian symbol.
a. Name two ceremonies in which water is used.
b. Write down three things that the use of water in these ceremonies suggests to you.

5 Religious symbols

Jewish symbols

The Jewish faith is rich in symbols and many of them play an important part in Jewish life and worship. Since Jews believe it is equally important to worship God in the home as it is in the synagogue, many symbols are found in both places.

Symbols in the home

Judaism provides guidelines that cover every aspect of daily life. Most Jews, for example, follow a dietary code covering all the food they eat, which is laid down in the Torah. These laws say that Jews can eat only:

- animals that chew the cud and have completely parted hooves
- birds such as chicken, duck and turkey
- fish with fins and scales.

Food that is permitted is called **kosher** ('fit'). Kosher food is a symbol of the purity and obedience that God asks of all Jews. The same rules also apply to the way in which food is prepared and cooked, as well as which items can be eaten with which. Kosher is a daily reminder of the importance of obeying the Torah.

A Jewish men always wear a tallit when they pray

The mezuzah is another important symbol in a Jewish home. This is a small handwritten scroll containing the Shema. It is placed in a decorative case and attached to the doorposts of most of the rooms in the house. Some people lightly kiss the fingertips of their right hand and touch the case of the mezuzah as they go in and out of each room. By doing this they are showing their respect for the Torah and its teaching, symbolised by the scroll.

Symbols in the synagogue

Among the most important symbols found in a synagogue are the Ark and the Everlasting Light that burns above it. The Ark is the holiest part of the synagogue because it houses the scrolls of the Torah. The Everlasting Light is a reminder that God is always with them, as well as reminding them of the lamp that burned continuously in the old Temple in Jerusalem. This light was finally extinguished by the Romans in 70 CE when they destroyed the Temple. To some Jews the Everlasting Light is also a symbol of the spiritual light which, they believe, flows out of the holy city.

Several important symbols are used by Jewish men when they pray. The head is covered by a small skull-cap; the two boxes of the tefillin, containing the Shema, are worn on the forehead and the left arm; and a white shawl, called the tallit, is draped around the shoulders.

Also visible somewhere in the synagogue is the Star of David. This star is made up of two equilateral triangles, one pointing upwards and the other downwards. No one is quite sure how this symbol came to be associated with the old Jewish king, David. Known as the 'magen David', it was incorporated into the flag of Israel when that country was founded in 1948.

Religious symbols 5

B A mezuzah on the doorpost of most rooms in a Jewish home symbolises the presence of God in the house

C The menorah and the Star of David are two of the most important Jewish symbols

In the glossary
Kosher

Find the answers
- What name is given to the food that a Jew is allowed to eat?
- What is written on the scroll found inside a mezuzah?
- What burns over the Ark in a synagogue?

Learning about, learning from

1. **a.** What does kosher mean?
   b. Why is kosher food a symbol and what does it symbolise?

2. **a.** What is a mezuzah?
   b. Where would you be likely to find one in a Jewish home?
   c. What do many Jewish people do to the mezuzah as they enter and leave a room?
   d. What does a mezuzah remind Jews of?

3. Imagine a Jewish friend is coming to your home for a meal. Using books from the library and/or the internet, find out as much as you can about the kosher laws and plan a three-course meal for you both to enjoy.

Extra activity
Some Jewish people believe that the Everlasting Light symbolises the belief that the light of the Torah will shine for ever. Look up Psalm 119.5 and explain what you think this means.

85

5 Religious symbols

Muslim symbols

The main visible symbols of Islam are the crescent moon and star which are found on every mosque. Both the moon and the stars are traditionally important in the Middle East, the homeland of Islam, as they help to guide desert people travelling by night. The Prophet Muhammad grew up in a city where the moon and the stars were worshipped but he attacked this as idolatry. They were, however, suitable symbols for Islam because the faith is believed to guide mankind (the star) and to light the way of every believer through a dark world (the moon).

The dome and the minarets

It is an important belief in Islam that, while the imam may lead the prayers in the mosque, each person enters the presence of God on their own. The shape and design of a mosque is planned to help worshippers concentrate their minds on God. The dome and the minarets are among its most noticeable features. The dome symbolises the heavens and the universe which Allah created and over which he reigns for ever. The minarets are towers from where the mu'adhin calls the faithful to prayer five times each day. The call and the minaret act as a beacon, bringing light into a dark world. There are usually four minarets on large mosques and, together with the dome, they remind worshippers of the **Five Pillars** of Islam. These pillars are the main guidelines by which each Muslim lives his or her life:

- **Shahadah** – the declaration of faith in Allah (see the box on the next page).
- **Salah** – prayer five times a day.
- **Zakah** – giving $2\frac{1}{2}$ per cent of income to help the needy and the poor.
- **Sawm** – fasting during the daylight hours of the festival of Ramadan each year.
- **Hajj** – pilgrimage to the holy city of Makkah.

Prayer as a symbol

As long as he or she is in a clean place, Muslims can pray anywhere. All prayer begins with wudu, a ritual for cleansing the body thoroughly. If running water is not available for this, clean sand will do just as well. The washing process symbolises the purity that Allah expects of everyone who comes into His presence to worship. During the prayer ritual, Muslims must prostrate themselves (bow down) in God's presence. God is almighty and all-powerful. A kneeling position with the forehead touching the floor is an appropriate position for a worshipper to adopt. It symbolises an acceptance of who God is and of the total sinfulness of all human beings.

A This man is bowing low before Allah as he prays

Religious symbols 5

In the glossary
Five Pillars   Sawm
Hajj   Shahadah
Salah   Zakah

Find the answers
- What are the main symbols of Islam?
- Who calls the faithful to prayer five times a day in a mosque?
- What are minarets?

Learning about, learning from
1. The crescent moon and star are important symbols in Islam. Why are they suitable symbols?
2. A Muslim must wash himself before he prays and prostrate himself during prayer. Why are these actions important and what do they mean?
3. a. What are the Five Pillars of Islam?
   b. Would it be helpful for you to have clear guidelines by which to live your own life?
   c. What guidelines would you like to see other people live by? Explain your answer.

B The crescent moon, an important Muslim symbol, is seen above this mosque

The Shahadah
There is no God but Allah and Muhammad is the messenger of Allah.

Extra activity
'The Muslim faith is full of symbols because of what Muslims believe about God.' Explain what this statement means.

5 Religious symbols

Hindu symbols

In the Hindu faith, everything that exists is part of **Brahman**, the Supreme Spirit. Everything can be used to help to focus a Hindu's mind on God during worship. The images of God (murtis) found in Hindu temples and elsewhere are not themselves worshipped. They do, however, point the worshipper to the Supreme Spirit with whom, after many rebirths, each Hindu hopes to be reunited. Only when this happens is a Hindu's life on earth complete.

There are thought to be about 330 million Hindu gods. Most families worship one in particular, whose murti has a sacred place in their home. Each person finds their murti to be full of symbolism and through understanding this they are able to worship Brahman. We can see this if we look at one popular Hindu god – Ganesha, the elephant-headed god.

Ganesha

For the past 1000 years Ganesha, the son of the gods **Shiva** and Parvati, has been one of the most popular Hindu gods. One legend explains why he has the head of an elephant. Shiva was away from home for a long time and Parvati made a model of a boy from mud and brought him to life to keep her company. The boy guarded the path to the river where Parvati bathed each day. Shiva returned unexpectedly and was so annoyed when the young boy stood in his way that he killed him. He was heartbroken to learn later that he had killed his own son. He told his servant to visit earth and to bring back the first head that he found to fit on the boy's shoulders. The servant returned with the head of an elephant.

The murti of Ganesha is full of symbolism, as are most statues of the gods:

- He has four hands. In two hands he holds a string of beads and a stick. The beads are a symbol of Ganesha's control over death and the stick is used to make each human being behave properly. In his other two hands are an axe to destroy ignorance and sweets to reward those whose ignorance has been taken away.
- Around the neck of Ganesha is a snake worn as a necklace. In many religions the snake is a symbol of evil. Here Ganesha is in perfect control of the snake and so is able to offer human beings the power to conquer evil.
- Ganesha sits on a mouse. As Ganesha is a powerful elephant, this shows his concern for all life, both great and small.

The sacred syllable

From Ganesha's mouth comes the most sacred of Hindu words and its most important symbol, **aum**. This is made up of three sounds that represent:

- the three Vedas – the ancient Hindu holy books

A Ganesha is the Hindu god of strength and wisdom

88

Religious symbols 5

B This is the Hindu symbol representing the sacred syllable of aum

- the three worlds – the earth, the atmosphere and heaven
- the three main Hindu gods – **Brahma**, **Vishnu** and Shiva.

The sacred syllable is believed to contain all the secrets of the universe. It is chanted before reading the Hindu scriptures, prayer, meditation and any act of worship.

From the Upanishads

The Upanishads, a Hindu sacred book, says this about aum:
Aum. The imperishable sound is the seed of all that exists. The past, the present and the future are all but the unfolding of aum... Meditation on this sacred syllable satisfies every need and finally leads to liberation.

In the glossary
Aum Shiva
Brahma Vishnu
Brahman

Find the answers
- What does a Hindu eventually hope to reach?
- What is a murti?
- Who chopped off the head of his son and replaced it with that of an elephant?

Learning about, learning from

1 In your own words, describe the legend that explains why Ganesha has the head of an elephant.

2 Murtis of Ganesha contain many symbols. Explain what each of these symbols mean.
   a. The four hands.
   b. The necklace.
   c. The mouse on which Ganesha sits.

3 Hindu children are often given the names of gods or goddesses. What do their parents hope to achieve for their children by doing this?

Extra activity
How might a murti help a Hindu in his or her worship?

89

5 Religious symbols

Sikh symbols

A Here you can see the Sikh symbol on either side of the takht, the throne on which the Guru Granth Sahib sits in the gurdwara

Sikhism is more than just a belief in God, as important as that is. It is a community of believers, a fellowship and a brotherhood. Sikhs can offer up their prayers at any time but they should also meet regularly with other Sikhs for worship together. You can read what the Guru Granth Sahib says about this in the box on the next page.

The gurdwara as a symbol

The gurdwara, the Sikh place of worship, symbolises the unity that exists between all Sikhs worldwide. This unity is expressed for all to see by the flag – the nishan sahib – that flies over every gurdwara. This announces that the building is a place set aside for the worship of God. Three symbols are found on the triangular flag:

- Two kirpans – short swords which are part of the Five Ks.
- A circle.
- The **khanda** – a double-edged sword.

These are the most important symbols of Sikhism and are taken from army life. This is because the Sikh sees himself as a holy warrior, serving God and fighting against the forces of evil. In the past Sikhs have often been called upon to take up the sword to defend their faith. Another khanda is placed at the top of the flagpole to emphasise this. In modern times the battle is much more likely to be a spiritual one against the forces opposed to God.

The Five Ks

The Khalsa is a fellowship of committed Sikhs. Not every Sikh joins the Khalsa but those who do are given the Five Ks as symbols of their commitment to God. They are as follows:

- **Kesh** – long hair. Uncut hair is a symbol of dedication to God and religious faith.
- **Kangha** – a comb. This is needed to keep the hair clean and tidy. It is a symbol of the physical and spiritual cleanliness that God expects of every Sikh.
- **Kara** – a steel band worn around the right wrist. It shows that the wearer is faithful to the teachings of the Gurus. The circle of the bracelet symbolises the eternity and unity of all Sikhs, which cannot be broken.
- **Kachs** – traditional underwear/shorts. Kachs are a symbol that the person is always ready to fight for the faith.
- **Kirpan** – a short sword. This is a symbol of the power and freedom of Sikhism. Each member of the Khalsa is a spiritual warrior.

The Guru Granth Sahib and ik oankar

The holy book, the Guru Granth Sahib, is the most important symbol in Sikhism. Every building that contains a copy of the book is a gurdwara. No service can be

Religious symbols 5

held without the Guru Granth Sahib being present. The reason for this is clear. The holy book is a symbol of the presence of God.

One other symbol is also important – the **ik oankar**. This means 'there is only one God' and it is the first line of the Mool Mantar, the poem of praise to God that comes at the beginning of the Guru Granth Sahib.

B The flag outside every gurdwara is a sign of the Sikh presence in the community

From the Guru Granth Sahib

The Sikh holy book says this about the gurdwara:
The highest and the most beneficial deed is the Lord's praise in the holy congregation [meeting together for worship in the gurdwara]. Holy congregation is the school of the True Guru [God]. There we learn to love God and appreciate his goodness.

In the glossary
Ik oankar	Kara
Kachs	Kesh
Kangha	Khanda

Find the answers
- What is the name of the flag outside every gurdwara?
- What is the brotherhood called to which many Sikhs belong?
- Which five symbols are worn by members of the Khalsa?

Learning about, learning from
1. **a.** What is the nishan sahib?
   b. Draw and label a picture of the nishan sahib flying on a flagpole.
2. The khanda is at the centre of the flag which flies outside every gurdwara. What is the khanda and what does it symbolise?
3. Sikh believe that they are called by God to fight against the forces of evil in the world. What forces of evil are there in the modern world?

Extra activity
Read the extract from the Guru Granth Sahib in the box.
a. Why is God called the 'True Guru'?
b. What is a congregation and to what does it refer in the extract?
c. Why is this congregation called 'holy'?
d. Why is the holy congregation called the 'school of the True Guru'?

5 Religious symbols

Buddhist symbols

The three most important symbols in Buddhism are the eight-spoked wheel, the lotus flower and the statue of the Buddha.

The eight-spoked wheel

The wheel is the main symbol of Buddhism. Its eight spokes are a reminder that the teaching of the Buddha is summed up in the Eight-Fold Path. This sets out the Middle Way – the life that a Buddhist should live between a life of luxury and a life of total self-denial. The Middle Way involves:

- holding a right viewpoint on life – the viewpoint of the Buddha
- thinking about life in the right way
- speaking in a helpful and thoughtful way – one that helps and supports others
- acting in the right way – following the example of the Buddha
- earning one's living in a way that does not harm, hurt or offend others
- putting in the right amount of effort needed to live a good life
- being aware of all that is needed to live a good life
- using meditation as a means of achieving all these things.

The lotus flower

The lotus flower is an important Buddhist symbol. The roots of this flower grow in muddy water but the petals rise up out of the water and open towards the sun. This symbolises the growth of every Buddhist towards spiritual fulfilment. People may start in the mud of greed and ignorance but they can grow to be loving and kind by following the Buddha's teachings.

Worshippers sometimes cup their hands together as they pray to symbolise the lotus flower. Just as the lotus flower comes in many different colours, so there are many different kinds of people seeking spiritual enlightenment. Everyone, however, must follow the same path – the Middle Way.

The Buddha

The 'Buddha' means 'the enlightened one'. Although there have been thousands of buddhas (spiritual teachers), the statues are always of Siddhartha Gotama, the first person to be enlightened. Although he can be shown in many different positions, such as standing up or lying down, he is often shown in the 'lotus position'. In this

A Images of the Buddha are full of symbolism

Religious symbols 5

B The eight-spoked wheel reminds Buddhists of the Middle Way

position the thumb and first finger of one hand form a circle. This symbolises the first teachings that he gave to his followers. A bump on the top of his head shows that he has been given special powers. A 'third eye' in the middle of his forehead symbolises the belief that the Buddha can 'see' things that no one else 'sees'. The Buddha's long ear lobes show that he came from an important family and his curled hair reveals that he was a holy man.

The lotus flower

From an old Buddhist book:
Just as the lotus, though it is born in the water, yet remains undefiled by the water, just so should the strenuous monk, earnest in effort, remain undefiled.

Find the answers

- What is the lotus position?
- What does the word 'Buddha' mean?
- Who was the first person to be enlightened?

Learning about, learning from

1. **a.** Why is the eight-spoked wheel an important Buddhist symbol?
   b. Why do Buddhists try to follow the Eight-Fold Path?
   c. Read the points in the Eight-Fold Path. What do you think of these rules? Could you live by them? Which ones would you find the most difficult to keep? Explain your answers.

2. Buddhists follow the example of the Buddha by keeping to the Middle Way. What do they mean by this and why is it given this name?

3. Explain the symbol of the lotus flower and what it means for a Buddhist.

4. If you were asked to write down your own keys to future happiness, what items would you include in your list?

Extra activity

The Buddha suggested that the path to true happiness was to be found midway between luxury and total self-denial. Do you think this is true for people today? Explain your answer.

93

6 Holy places

Introduction

A pilgrimage is a holy journey undertaken by followers of a religion to a holy place. Some people go on such a journey because of the deep spiritual peace that it can bring to them. Others use a pilgrimage to deepen their religious faith. Many pilgrims travel for the experience of meeting others who hold similar beliefs to their own. Many go in search of healing from some disease or illness. Some pilgrims go looking for forgiveness from their sins. In some religions, such as Islam, pilgrimage is a solemn obligation for all Muslims, while in other religions, such as Christianity, it is an option but no more.

The city of Jerusalem

The holy city of Jerusalem is sacred for Jews, Muslims and Christians. When the Jewish Temple was still standing in Jerusalem 2000 years ago, all Jews were expected to visit the city three times a year for the great 'pilgrimage' festivals – **Passover**, Shavuot and Sukkoth. The only part of the old Temple left standing is the Western Wall, which is still visited by thousands of Jewish pilgrims each year. It was also in Jerusalem that the earthly life of Jesus came to a sudden end. Thousands of Christian pilgrims visit the city each year, especially during the festivals of **Christmas** and Easter. For Muslims the city is the third most important holy site after Makkah and **Madinah**.

Hindu holy places

There are many holy places in Hinduism and worshippers are likely to visit them many times. Often the main reason for the journey is for them to meet their guru (spiritual teacher). Although there are many holy places in the mountainous areas of India, Hindus have long regarded rivers as the most holy places of all. This is particularly true of those places were two rivers meet, such as at **Varanasi**.

Christian holy places

Thousands of Christians make a pilgrimage each year. The most popular destination is Palestine, the Holy Land, and the places there associated with Jesus. Many Christians also travel to such places as Lourdes in France and Walsingham in England, both of which are associated with visions of the Virgin Mary.

Muslim holy places

All fit and healthy Muslims are expected to make a pilgrimage to the holy city of Makkah – a journey called the Hajj – at least once in their lifetime. This is one of the Five Pillars of Islam. On the journey many of them also visit other places that are important in Muslim history. Those who are unable to go can financially support someone who is making the journey or pay for someone else to go in their place.

94

In this unit

In this unit you will read about the following:

- The city of Jerusalem, a city which is holy to the followers of Judaism, Christianity and Islam.
- Christian holy places, both those in the Holy Land of Israel and those associated with various saints, especially the Virgin Mary.
- The Hajj – the pilgrimage undertaken by all fit Muslims to the cities of Makkah and Madinah.
- Hindu pilgrimages to such holy places as rivers, mountains and towns associated with visits to earth by the gods.
- The Sikh holy city of Amritsar, the home of the Golden Temple.
- Buddhist holy places including **stupas** – places that held the cremation ashes of the Buddha or have become holy places since.

The Hajj

In the Qur'an all Muslims are told that they must go on a pilgrimage to Makkah at some time:

*Exhort all men to make the pilgrimage. They will come on foot and on the backs of swift camels and from every quarter. Let the pilgrims spruce themselves, make their vows and circle the Ancient House [the **Ka'bah**]. Such is Allah's commandment. He that reveres the sacred rites of Allah shall fare better in the sight of the Lord.*

In the glossary

Christmas   Passover
Ka'bah   Stupas
Madinah   Varanasi

6 Holy places

Jerusalem

Jerusalem is a very important city to Jews, Christians and Muslims. It was here that King David, the most important Jewish king, made his capital city and where his son, Solomon, built his first great Temple in 950 BCE. It was also here that Jesus was crucified. The city contains many places that are sacred to Judaism, Christianity and Islam.

The Western Wall

Solomon's Temple was destroyed in 586 BCE and after a period of some 500 years a replacement was built by King Herod the Great. The Romans destroyed this Temple in 70 CE and it was never rebuilt. All that remains now of Herod's Temple is the Western Wall, also known as the Wailing Wall. For hundreds of years Jewish pilgrims have prayed there, reciting the holy Torah and inserting their prayers in the cracks of the Wall. By doing this Jews are expressing their great sorrow that they are still scattered throughout their world. Although Jews now have their own country, Israel, there are far more Jews living outside Israel than within it. They are praying for God's blessing on the Jewish community and looking forward to the coming of the Messiah, God's promised deliverer, who will defeat the enemies of Israel.

Christians and Jerusalem

For Christians, Jerusalem is a very special city associated with the life and death of Jesus. As a Jew, and knowing that his death was near, Jesus made his way to the city. There was a very old tradition that Jerusalem was the only suitable place for a prophet to meet death. In the courtyard of the Roman governor, Pontius Pilate, Jesus was tried and sentenced to death. In the same city, three days later, his disciples rejoiced at the news that God had brought him back to life.

Christian pilgrims can visit the city at any time but most travel there during the days leading up to the great festival of Easter. On Good Friday they follow in the footsteps of Jesus by walking along the Via Dolorosa ('the way of sorrows'). Some pilgrims carry a cross on their shoulders just as Jesus did 2000 years ago. They also visit the Church of the Holy Sepulchre, which is built where the tomb of Jesus is believed to have been.

Muslims in Jerusalem

After Makkah and Madinah, Jerusalem is the most holy city in Islam. The Dome of the Rock, a Muslim shrine, commemorates the Night Journey that the Prophet Muhammad made on a winged horse through the seven spheres of heaven to meet Allah. From Allah's presence, Muhammad returned to earth to preach the message he had received. It is this message that has persuaded millions of people over the centuries to become Muslims.

A The Western Wall, where thousands of Jews come to pray, is the most important Jewish pilgrimage destination

Holy places 6

B The mosque of the Dome of the Rock in Jerusalem is, after Makkah and Madinah, the most important holy site to Muslims

Jesus and Jerusalem

The Gospels tell of an occasion when Jesus was upset about the future of the city of Jerusalem. He said:

O Jerusalem, Jerusalem, you who kill the prophets and stone those sent to you, how often have I longed to gather your children together, as a hen gathers her chicks under her wings, but you were not willing. Look, your house is left to you desolate.

Find the answers

- Who built the original Temple in Jerusalem and when was it destroyed?
- What is the Western Wall?
- Which other cities, apart from Jerusalem, are holy to Muslims?

Learning about, learning from

1 Explain in two sentences why the city of Jerusalem is important to each of the following people.
   a. Jews.
   b. Christians.
   c. Muslims.

2 Using books from the library and/or the internet, find out as much as you can about the city of Jerusalem. Try to find pictures of the Western Wall, the Church of the Holy Sepulchre and the Dome of the Rock mosque. Use the information to write a short project on Jerusalem in your exercise book or file.

3 Imagine you are praying at the Western Wall or visiting Jerusalem as a Christian pilgrim. Explain why you are in the city and what you are doing.

Extra activity

Despite the many beliefs they have in common, Jews, Christians and Muslims have not always been on friendly terms. Some believers think Jerusalem should be for *their* religion and no other. Others think the holy sites should be shared out. How would you begin to solve this problem?

6 Holy places

Christian holy places

Christian pilgrims visit holy places for a number of reasons:

- To give thanks for something that God or a saint is believed to have done for them.
- To say a special prayer asking for help.
- To seek healing.
- To express repentance for wrong-doing and to seek God's forgiveness.

Christian holy places can be put into two groups:

- Those in the Holy Land of Israel where the events in the life of Jesus took place. These include the villages of Bethlehem and Nazareth, where Jesus was born and grew up, and the city of Jerusalem where he died.
- Those that are associated with saints, for example where they are buried or believed to have seen visions.

Pilgrimages in Britain

The most well-known Christian pilgrimage site in Britain is at Walsingham in Norfolk. In 1061 the lady of the manor, Richeldis de Faverches, had three visions of the Virgin Mary. In her visions she was transported to a house in Nazareth and told to build an exact replica of it in Walsingham. It was destroyed in the sixteenth century but rebuilt in 1931. Anglicans, Roman Catholics and Orthodox Christians now have their own shrines in this small town and thousands of pilgrims travel there each year.

Pilgrimages overseas

In Europe there are many places where Christian pilgrims have travelled to in the past and still do so today. With its many links with the early Christian Church, the city of Rome receives many visitors. During festival times, especially at Easter, Christians gather in St Peter's Square to receive the Pope's blessing. Pilgrims also visit the home of St Francis in Assisi. This thirteenth-century saint was famous for his love of birds and animals.

Other pilgrims undertake a journey to seek healing. It was at Lourdes in 1850 that a 14-year-old girl called Bernadette Soubrier had 18 visions of the Virgin Mary. A spring of water appeared and miraculous healings are said to have taken place. About two million people each year visit Lourdes and many of them are sick or disabled. Even though only a small number are thought to have been physically healed, most return from their visit to Lourdes with a deep sense of God's love and peace.

A Walsingham is the most important pilgrimage destination in Britain

Holy places 6

B The Pope blesses people in St Peter's Square, a traditional Christian pilgrimage destination

Walsingham

This description comes from a guidebook for pilgrims in Walsingham:

The pilgrimage begins with what is known as the First Visit. Pilgrims assemble outside the Holy House. There the story of what took place in the first Holy House in Nazareth is read. Pilgrims listen again to the good news announced by the angel of the Lord to Mary. They hear her 'Yes' in response to God's invitation to become the mother of Jesus Christ His Son.

'I am the handmaid of the Lord,' she said, 'be it unto me according to your word.'

A procession is then formed and makes its way into the Holy House itself. Very often Mary's own hymn – the Magnificat – is said or sung as it does so.

Find the answers

- Why do Christian pilgrims go to Bethlehem, Nazareth and Jerusalem?
- What led to the building of a shrine at Walsingham?
- Which pilgrimage site was established after the visions of a 14-year-old girl?

Learning about, learning from

1. **a.** List three important centres of Christian pilgrimage and describe one of them.
   b. Using books from the library and/or the internet, find out more about another Christian pilgrimage site not explained on these pages.

2. **a.** Do you like going on special journeys?
   b. What makes a journey interesting for you?
   c. Would you like to go on a Christian pilgrimage? What do you think might make the pilgrimage especially interesting?

3. Read the extract about Walsingham in the box. Why do many people find it helpful to visit places associated with the Virgin Mary?

Extra activity

Many pilgrims who go to Lourdes say they come back physically unchanged but spiritually blessed. What do they mean by this?

6 Holy places

Makkah

All healthy Muslims, male and female, must make the Hajj – the annual pilgrimage to the holy city of Makkah – at least once in their lifetime. It is one of the Five Pillars of Islam. The pilgrimage must take place during the month of Ramadan, during which Muslims throughout the world are expected to fast during daylight hours. Each year about two million pilgrims make their way to Makkah from all over the world.

In Makkah

As they reach the outskirts of Makkah, male pilgrims put on two pieces of cloth to symbolise ihram, the state of purity entered into by those making the Hajj. They call out: 'We have come in answer to your call, O Lord.'

Once in the city each pilgrim performs the tawaf by walking seven times (three times quickly and four times slowly) around the Ka'bah. Moving in an anti-clockwise direction, and always keeping the Ka'bah to his left, each pilgrim tries to kiss the Black Stone at the base of the Ka'bah. This stone is believed to have been given by Allah to Ibrahim (Abraham). It was once white but has been turned black by the sins of the human race.

Outside Makkah

You can see from picture A the route pilgrims take on leaving Makkah. It was between Safa and Marwa that Isma'il's mother ran frantically to and fro looking for water, only to discover that her young son had already been shown a well in the desert by God. To relive this event, pilgrims run the 366 metres between the two places seven times.

The following day, after sunrise, the pilgrims set out for Mount Arafat. Some walk and others ride. Once there, the pilgrims offer prayers, remembering the words of Muhammad: '[that] the best of prayers is that of the day of Arafat.'

After spending the night in the open, the pilgrims collect 49 stones on their way to Mina. Once there, they throw the stones at three stone pillars. These pillars represent the devil and remind pilgrims that Isma'il was tempted by the devil to rebel against his father, Ibrahim. It is believed that Isma'il drove the devil away by throwing stones at him.

Id-ul-Adha

The festival of **Id-ul-Adha** held at Mina ends the Hajj. It is celebrated by all Muslims whether they are on the pilgrimage or not. It commemorates Ibrahim's willingness to sacrifice his first-born son to God. Muslims make the

A This picture shows the route followed by pilgrims on the Hajj

Holy places 6

sacrifice of an animal, usually a sheep. In this way Muslims everywhere are sharing in the blessings that all those who have taken part in the pilgrimage have enjoyed.

B The Ka'bah, the shrine in the middle of Makkah, is the main destination of all pilgrims on the Hajj

From the Qur'an

Muslims make the Hajj because God tells them to do so through the words of the Qur'an:
Make the pilgrimage and visit the Sacred House for His sake... Make the pilgrimage in the appointed month.

In the glossary
Id-ul-Adha

Find the answers
- Who is expected to go on the Hajj?
- When does the Hajj take place?
- Where is the Black Stone believed to have come from?

Learning about, learning from

1. When pilgrims enter Makkah they call out: 'We have come in answer to your call, O Lord.' This sums up the real reason for going on the Hajj. What is it?

2. a. Why do Muslim pilgrims on the Hajj throw stones at three stone pillars?
   b. How did the devil tempt Ismai'l?

3. What does the festival of Id-ul-Adha celebrate?

4. Muslims describe the Hajj as 'the journey of a lifetime'. What would make a journey one of a lifetime for you?

Extra activity

a. It is said that one of the spiritual benefits of undertaking the Hajj is that it purges pilgrims of their pride. How might the pilgrimage to Makkah do this?

b. How do you think this kind of pride might show itself in a person's life?

101

6 Holy places

Hindu pilgrimages

India is a country known for its many holy places. Among them are rivers, mountains and holy towns.

Rivers

There are seven sacred rivers in India and the River Ganges is the most holy of them all. Hindus believe that bathing in one of these rivers removes all bad karma. After death, to have your ashes sprinkled on the waters frees you from the cycle of birth, death and rebirth in which everyone is caught up. The source of a river or the place where two rivers meet are considered particularly holy.

Mountains

Mountains, particularly the high peaks of the Himalayas, are believed to be holy. Traditional Hindu stories taught that the gods made their homes in these mountains. Struggling to reach the home of Shiva in the mountains is believed by many Hindus to bring great merit.

Holy towns

The holiest Hindu town is Varanasi. This place is special because of its location on the banks of the River Ganges, close to where the river meets its smaller tributary, the Varuna. Varanasi is particularly holy because of the Hindu belief that the great god Shiva lived there. The city attracts a million pilgrims each year, who between them visit more than 1000 temples in the town which are dedicated to Shiva alone. The most important of these temples is the Golden Temple, which was built in 1783. Hindu pilgrims regard every stone in this temple as holy. Shiva is the Hindu god of life, death and rebirth. He is the visible form of the power who both creates life and destroys it. He is often portrayed in statues as taking part in a world-shattering dance.

Ghats

Along the three-mile stretch of the River Ganges in Varanasi there are steps called ghats. Hindu pilgrims use these to bathe in the sacred waters of the Ganges. Bathing here cleanses the body after a long journey but, more importantly, it cleanses the soul of all evil. Some Hindus bathe in the icy waters close to the source of the Ganges. Huge bathing fairs, called 'melas', are held every 12 years in the Ganges and elsewhere, which attract millions of pilgrims.

The cremation of dead bodies is carried out on the ghats and sacred marigold leaves are scattered on the waters of the river. It is the dearest wish of every Hindu to die in Varanasi and to have their ashes scattered there. They believe this guarantees that their soul will pass

A Shiva is the Hindu god of life, death and rebirth

Holy places 6

straight to Brahman without needing to be reborn again. This is extremely important in Hinduism, which believes strongly in reincarnation.

Hindus also often go on a pilgrimage because they have asked their god for a particular favour in the past and their prayers have been answered. They feel that they want to visit the shrine of that particular god to give thanks and express their devotion to him in the future.

The River Ganges

A modern traveller has written the following about the River Ganges:
It is great because, to millions of Hindus, it is the most sacred, venerated [honoured] river on earth. To bathe in it is to wash away guilt. To drink the water, having bathed in it, and to carry away bottles of it for those who have not had the great fortune to make the pilgrimage, is meritorious [praiseworthy]. To be cremated on its banks, having died there, is the wish of every Hindu. Even to call out 'Ganga, Ganga' at the distance of 55 kilometres from the river makes amends for the sins committed during three previous lives.

B Hindu pilgrims bathe in the River Ganges so that their sins may be forgiven

Learning about, learning from

1. **a.** How many sacred rivers are there in India?
   b. Which mountain range is particularly holy to Hindus?
   c. Why do you think rivers and mountains have become holy to Hindus?
   d. Why is the town of Varanasi thought to be particularly holy?

2. Picture B shows ghats along the banks of the River Ganges. What might a visitor to the city of Varanasi see as he or she walks along the river bank?

3. Imagine you are a young Hindu visiting Varanasi for the first time. What effect might the experience have upon you?

Find the answers

- Which river is the most holy in India?
- What is the name for the Hindu belief in life after death?
- Which god is most closely associated with Varanasi?

Extra activity

Why do you think people from many different religions find it spiritually rewarding to visit holy places such as Varanasi?

6 Holy places

Amritsar

Guru Nanak taught his followers that a pilgrimage is only valuable if a person is in a good spiritual frame of mind before the journey begins. The journey will only draw the pilgrim closer to God if he or she is willing to give up their evil ways and change the way they are living. If the pilgrim is willing to change, they may join the thousands of pilgrims making their way to the Golden Temple in Amritsar, confident that God will bless them.

Building the Golden Temple

It was Guru Ram Das who began to build the city of Amritsar in 1573. During this work the builders extended a natural pool into a lake called the 'pool of nectar', so that Sikhs could bathe in it. Guru Arjan, the youngest son of Guru Ram Das, built a temple in the middle of the lake, which became known as the Harimandir ('temple of God'). The foundation stone of the Harimandir was laid by a Muslim in 1589, the building was completed in 1601 and the Adi Granth was installed in 1604. In the nineteenth century a Sikh ruler covered the top part of the building with gold leaf and it became known as the Golden Temple.

B Most Sikhs hope to make at least one visit to the Golden Temple

The Golden Temple

The Golden Temple is the most important building in Sikhism. It stands on a platform just 20 metres square in the middle of a large artificial lake. It was built with four entrances to show that everyone was welcome to enter it. Verses from the Guru Granth Sahib are carved into the walls and very old copies of the holy book are stored inside. The holy book is at the centre of life in the Golden Temple, as it is in every gurdwara. Readings from it begin at dawn and continue until late at night. Ragis (musicians) play and sing continually. A small hall of mirrors makes the walls even more beautiful and underline the importance of the Guru Granth Sahib. In the past only an important emperor could have afforded such luxury. At the end of

A Since the Golden Temple was built by Guru Arjan it has been at the heart of Sikhism

Holy places 6

each day the Guru Granth Sahib is carried in procession to the room where it is stored for the night. It is a great honour for a Sikh to be invited to take part in this procession.

Over the gateway to the Temple is the treasury, where there used to be four sets of golden doors, jewelled canopies and umbrellas, and the golden spades that were used to begin the desilting of the lake in 1923. All these items were destroyed when the Indian Army invaded the Golden Temple complex in 1984 to put down an armed uprising.

Entering the Golden Temple

As in all gurdwaras, worshippers entering the Golden Temple remove their shoes and cover their heads. They wash their feet before entering the outer area. They bow as they enter the Harimandir, leave their gifts just inside the rail and receive the holy food of karah parshad before they leave. Many worshippers also visit the nearby museum before leaving the Temple complex because it contains many important historical Sikh objects.

C Pilgrims visit the Golden Temple mainly to hear the continual reading of the Guru Granth Sahib

Find the answers
- Where is the Golden Temple?
- What is the 'pool of nectar'?
- What is the Harimandir?

Learning about, learning from

1. Design a poster to tell young Sikhs about the Golden Temple. Your poster should include a drawing of the holy building.

2. Imagine you are a Sikh visiting the Golden Temple for the first time. Write a letter to your family telling them about your visit.

3. What do you think people today, Sikhs and non-Sikhs, could learn from the fact that the Golden Temple has four entrances?

Extra activity

a. It was Guru Arjan who set the Harimandir in the middle of a large lake. What reasons might he have had for doing this?

b. Why is the lake in which the Harimandir stands called the 'pool of nectar'?

105

6 Holy places

Buddhist holy places

Buddhist pilgrims often visit places where the Buddha lived and taught. They hope that by following in the Master's footsteps they will be helped in their own search for spiritual enlightenment. Among the most popular places visited by Buddhist pilgrims are Lumbini, Bodh Gaya and stupas.

Lumbini

Siddhartha Gotama was born at Lumbini, in the foothills of the Himalayas, about 2500 years ago. This town is now in the country of Nepal. A community of Buddhist monks live in the town and there are many Buddhist temples there where people can meditate on their spiritual search. There is also a stone in the town that bears the inscription: 'Here the Buddha was born.'

Bodh Gaya

Bodh Gaya is the town in India where the Buddha gained spiritual enlightenment. There is a famous temple there called the Mahabodhi Temple ('great enlightenment temple'). There is also a descendant of the original tree under which the Buddha's enlightenment took place, together with many Buddhist symbols and works of art. Pieces of cloth decorate the tree and it is surrounded by lotus patterns and the wheel of the dhamma. Buddhist pilgrims travel to Bodh Gaya from all over the world.

Stupas

Stupas were originally chambers or burial mounds where the ashes of the Buddha were buried. The remains of the Buddha were divided into eight parts and a stupa was erected over each of them. Stupas were also built over the cremation urn and the ashes of the cremation fire. However, in the third century thousands of stupas were built to remind Buddhists of the teachings of the Buddha. Relics were taken to many countries where Buddhism was preached and stupas erected there. Some contain relics of a buddha or copies of the Buddhist scriptures. Many of them are pilgrimage destinations for Buddhists. When they visit a stupa pilgrims walk around it three times in a clockwise direction to remind themselves of the

A The temple at Bodh Gaya commemorates the enlightenment of the Buddha

Holy places 6

B Stupas were built over the places where the ashes of the Buddha were buried

In the glossary
Samsara   Three Jewels

Find the answers
- Why do Buddhist pilgrims often visit sites associated with the Buddha and what are they hoping for?
- Why is Lumbini an important Buddhist pilgrimage site?
- Why is Bodh Gaya important to Buddhists?

Three Jewels, the most important part of Buddhist teaching.

One of the most important stupas outside India is found at Borobudur, on the island of Java in Indonesia. Pilgrims there walk around the base of the great monument and then begin to climb the seven ascending terraces to reach the top. Their climb symbolises their progress along the path from **samsara** to nirvana. There are many carvings and statues on the way to remind them of their spiritual journey. When they reach the top, however, they are confronted with a simple solid stone stupa, which is in direct contrast to the many they have passed on their journey.

Sri Pada
Buddhist pilgrims often visit Sri Pada, a mountain in Sri Lanka. The mountain is particularly important for Buddhists because they believe it was visited by the Buddha. A stone at the summit of the mountain has marks on it, which look like footprints. Pilgrims believe they are the footprints of the Buddha.

Learning about, learning from
1. a. What is a stupa?
   b. How many stupas were originally built?
   c. Why were many more stupas built in India?
   d. What is special about the stupa at Borobudur in Java?

2. a. Why do Buddhist pilgrims particularly want to visit the place where the Buddha was spiritually enlightened?
   b. What are they are hoping to gain by visiting the town?

Extra activity
Relics are treated with great respect in many religions, including Christianity and Buddhism.
a. What is a relic?
b. Why are relics treated with such respect? What might their value be to followers of that religion?

107

Glossary

A

- **Abraham** — The person considered by Jews to be the father of the Jewish nation; Muslims believe him to be one of the prophets.
- **Absolution** — The pronouncement by a priest that a person's sins have been forgiven; most likely to happen in the Roman Catholic and some Anglican churches.
- **Adi Granth** — The original form of the Sikh scriptures before more was added to make it the Guru Granth Sahib.
- **Akhand Path** — The unbroken reading of the Guru Granth Sahib in the gurdwara; usually carried out on some special occasion.
- **Allah** — The name in Islam for God in the Arabic language.
- **Altar** — The raised platform at the eastern end of most churches, from where worship is conducted.
- **Amritsar** — The Sikh sacred city in the Punjab; home of the Golden Temple.
- **Anglican Church** — Churches worldwide which follow the teachings of the Church of England and which accept the leadership of the Archbishop of Canterbury.
- **Archbishops** — Senior priests in the Roman Catholic and Anglican Churches.
- **Ardas** — The most important Sikh prayer; draws every act of worship in the gurdwara to a close.
- **Ark** — The cabinet in the synagogue which houses the scrolls of the Torah; covered with a curtain when the scrolls are not in use.
- **Aum** — The Hindu sacred syllable; believed to contain the sound of all reality.
- **Avatars** — Visits of a Hindu god to earth in the form of a human being or an animal.

B

- **Baptism** — The service of initiation for most Christian Churches; linked with the washing away of sins.
- **Baptist Church** — Nonconformist Church; believes in the baptism of adults not children.
- **Believer's baptism** — The baptism of adults in the Baptist Church.
- **Bhagavad Gita** — A Hindu holy book.
- **Bible** — The Christian scriptures containing the Old and New Testaments; used by Christians in private and public worship.
- **Bishop** — A senior priest who carries the responsibility for all the churches in an area, ordains priests and performs confirmations.
- **Bodhissatva** — A Buddhist who becomes enlightened and then remains on earth to help others to reach enlightenment.
- **Brahma** — The Hindu Creator God.
- **Brahman** — The Supreme God in Hinduism; the holy power which runs through the whole universe.
- **Brahmins** — Members of the highest social group in Hindu society; priests are drawn from this group.
- **Breaking of Bread** — The name given to service of Holy Communion in many Nonconformist Churches.
- **Buddha** — Siddhartha Gotama, who became the Enlightened One; gave the teaching upon which Buddhism is based.

C

- **Cardinals** — Senior priests in the Roman Catholic Church.
- **Cathedral** — The main church in a diocese; contains the 'bishop's chair' from where the bishop conducts many of the services.
- **Celibacy** — The requirement not to marry or have any sexual relationships.
- **Chapel** — A small Nonconformist place of worship.
- **Chauri** — The fan which is waved over the Guru Granth Sahib in a Sikh gurdwara; made of yak hair or nylon and a symbol of the authority of the scriptures.
- **Chrismation** — The name given to service in the Orthodox Church in which a baby is both baptised and confirmed.
- **Christmas** — The Christian festival which is celebrated on 25 December; commemorates the birth of Jesus.
- **Church** — The building where Christians meet for worship.
- **Church of England** — The main Christian Church in Britain; also called the Anglican Church.

Glossary

	Citadels	Salvation Army places of worship.
	Confession	A sacrament of the Catholic Church; a meeting at which a priest hears a person's confession of sins and grants them God's forgiveness.
	Confirmation	A service in some Churches in which a person 'confirms' the promises that others made for them when they were baptised.
	Creeds	Traditional statements of Christian belief.
	Crucifix	A cross containing the body of Jesus.
D	Dhamma	The teachings of the Buddha.
	Divine Liturgy	The name given to the service of Holy Communion in the Orthodox Church.
E	Easter	The Christian festival at which believers remember and celebrate the death and resurrection of Jesus.
	Epistles	Letters in the New Testament written by Paul, Peter, John and others.
	Eucharist	The 'act of thanksgiving'; the name given in many Churches to the service of Holy Communion when the death of Jesus is remembered.
	Exodus	The journey out of Egyptian slavery taken by the Jews to the country of Canaan (Israel).
F	Five Ks	The five symbols given to all who become members of the Sikh Khalsa.
	Five Pillars	The five beliefs which form the foundation of Islam.
G	Ganesha	One of the most popular Hindu gods; has the head of an elephant.
	Golden Temple	The most holy building in Sikhism; built in the middle of a sacred pool in Amritsar between 1577 and 1589 CE.
	Good Friday	The day in the Christian year after Maundy Thursday when Christians remember the death of Jesus on the cross.
	Gospels	Four books at the beginning of the New Testament in the Bible; each Gospel describes the life and teaching of Jesus.
	Granthi	An official in a gurdwara who reads the Guru Granth Sahib many times a day; officiates at Sikh services and ceremonies.
	Gurdwara	'The doorway to the Guru'; the Sikh place of worship.
	Guru Gobind Singh	The last Sikh Guru (1666–1708 CE); founded the Khalsa brotherhood of Sikhs.
	Guru Granth Sahib	The Sikh scriptures, which were put together by Guru Arjan and completed by Guru Gobind Singh.
	Guru Nanak	The first Guru; the founder of the Sikh faith (1469–1539 CE).
	Gurus	Teachers; in Sikhism the title is used only for the ten human Gurus, for the Guru Granth Sahib and for God – the 'True Guru'.
H	Hajj	The annual pilgrimage to Makkah and other holy places which all Muslims are expected to undertake at least once in their lives.
	Havdalah	The service which draws the Sabbath Day to a close in a Jewish family; 'separates' the Sabbath Day from the rest of the week.
	Holy Communion	The service held in most Christian Churches to commemorate the death of Jesus; also called the Mass, Divine Liturgy, Eucharist and Lord's Supper.
	Holy Spirit	The third person in the Christian Trinity with God the Father and God the Son.
I	Id-ul-Adha	The Muslim festival commemorating the willingness of the prophet Ibrahim (Abraham) to sacrifice his son, Isma'il (Ishmael), to God.
	Ik oankar	The statement by Guru Nanak that God is one.
	Imam	The man who leads the prayers and preaches the Friday sermon in a mosque.
	Infant baptism	The practice of baptising babies; followed by most Churches including the Roman Catholic, Orthodox and Anglican Churches.
	Israel	Also called Palestine; the modern country of Israel was formed in 1948.

Glossary

J	Jerusalem	The city first captured by King David and the most sacred city to all Jews; it is also considered holy by Muslims and Christians.
K	Ka'bah	The cube-shaped shrine which stands in Makkah; visited by millions of pilgrims during the Hajj.
	Kachs	One of the Five Ks; shorts worn as an undergarment.
	Kangha	One of the Five Ks; a comb.
	Kara	One of the Five Ks; a steel bracelet.
	Karma	'Action' or 'deed'; the Hindu belief that what a person does in this life leads to rewards or punishments in the next life.
	Kesh	One of the Five Ks; uncut hair.
	Khalsa	The Sikh religious brotherhood open to male and female believers; begun by the tenth Guru, Guru Gobind Singh, in 1699 CE.
	Kirpan	One of the Five Ks; a short sword.
	Kosher	'Fit' or 'proper'; used to describe food which is judged fit to eat under Jewish dietary laws.
	Krishna	One of the most popular Hindu gods; an avatar of Vishnu.
L	Langar	'Guru's kitchen'; the dining hall in a gurdwara and the food served there.
	Lent	The season before Holy Week begins when Christians spend time in extra prayer and Bible study before the festival of Easter.
	Lord's Supper	The name given in some Nonconformist Churches to the celebration of Holy Communion.
M	Madinah	The city that welcomed Muhammad and his followers in 622 CE after he left Makkah.
	Mahabharata	The longest poem in the world; much loved as one of the Hindu sacred scriptures.
	Mahayana Buddhists	Followers of one of two main schools of Buddhism.
	Makkah	The birthplace of Muhammad in present-day Saudi Arabia.
	Mandir	The Hindu place of worship.
	Mantra	A sacred formula or chant; used particularly in Hindu worship.
	Martyrs	People who die for their religious beliefs.
	Mass	The name given by Roman Catholics to the service of Holy Communion.
	Menorah	The seven-branched candelabra which is a symbol in Judaism.
	Messiah	The figure expected by Jews to lead them out of captivity; Christians believe that Jesus was the promised Messiah.
	Methodist Church	The Nonconformist Church founded in the eighteenth century by John Wesley.
	Mezuzah	A small case containing passages from the Torah and attached to doorposts in Jewish homes.
	Mihrab	The niche in one wall of a mosque which indicates the direction of Makkah.
	Minaret	A tower outside a mosque.
	Minbar	A platform of steps from which the imam delivers his sermon in a mosque.
	Minister	A church leader in a Nonconformist Church.
	Monks	Men who devote themselves to a life of prayer and study; important in both Christianity and Buddhism.
	Mool Mantar	The statement of Sikh belief; the opening chapter of the Guru Granth Sahib.
	Moses	The man who led the Jews out of Egyptian slavery; received the Ten Commandments and the Jewish Law from God on Mount Sinai.
	Mosque	'Place of prostration'; the Muslim place of worship.
	Mu'adhin	The person who calls Muslims to prayer five times a day.
	Muhammad	The last, and greatest, prophet in Islam; the one chosen by Allah to receive the revelations which are collected in the Qur'an.
	Murti	A Hindu image or statue of God.

Glossary

N

	New Testament	The second part of the Christian Bible; it contains 27 books including the Gospels and the Epistles (letters) written by the early Christian leaders.
	Nirvana	The final state of perfect peace which all Buddhists strive for.
	Nonconformist Churches	Protestant Churches, such as the Baptist Church or Methodist Church, which separated from the Church of England in the seventeenth century.
	Nuns	Women who give themselves to a life of prayer, study and service; particularly important in Christianity and Buddhism.

O

	Old Testament	The Jewish scriptures included as the first part of the Christian Bible; contains 39 books.
	Ordination	The service which authorises men and women to work as priests.
	Orthodox Church	Originally the Church of the Eastern region of the Roman Empire; separated from the Roman Catholic Church in 1054 CE.

P

	Parables	Everyday stories told by Jesus which carry a spiritual or moral message.
	Passover	The Jewish festival which commemorates the delivery of the Jews from slavery in Egypt.
	Paul	The leader of the early Christian Church; a missionary and writer of many books in the New Testament.
	Peter	The main disciple of Jesus; became the first leader of the Christian Church after Jesus had left the earth.
	Pope	The head of the Roman Catholic Church; the Bishop of Rome.
	Priests	People ordained to the ministry in the Roman Catholic and Anglican Churches; given the authority to deliver the sacraments to the people.
	Prophet	A man or woman who passes on God's message to the people.
	Protestant Church	Churches which do not belong to the Roman Catholic or Orthodox Churches.
	Puja	A Hindu act of worship.

Q

	Quakers	The Christian Church formed in the seventeenth century by George Fox; known for its largely silent form of worship and also known as the Society of Friends.
	Qur'an	'That which is read or recited'; the divine book revealed to the Prophet Muhammad by Allah.

R

	Rabbis	Leaders of worship and teachers in a Jewish synagogue.
	Rak'ahs	Sequences of movements and prayers which make up the Muslim prayer routine.
	Ramadan	The ninth month of the Islamic calendar; during this month all Muslims must fast from daybreak until sunset.
	Ramayana	One of the Hindu holy books.
	Reformation	A sixteenth-century movement which broke away from Roman Catholic Church to form various Protestant Churches.
	Reincarnation	The belief held by Hindus and Buddhists that the soul is reborn many times before being released.
	Relics	The remains of a saint.
	Resurrection	The rising from the dead of Jesus on the third day after his crucifixion.
	Roman Catholic Church	The oldest Christian Church; owes its allegiance to the Pope in Rome.

S

	Sabbath Day	The seventh day of the week; a Jewish day of rest which lasts from Friday night to Saturday night.
	Sacraments	Special Christian services in which God's blessing is given through a physical object such as bread, wine, oil or water.
	Sadhus	Hindu holy men.
	Saints	Christians recognised for the holiness of their life.
	Salah	One of the Five Pillars of Islam; the formal prayers undertaken by Muslims and recited in Arabic five times a day.

Glossary

	Salvation Army	The Protestant Church founded in the nineteenth century; known for its social work as well as its services.
	Samsara	The wheel of rebirth; the world.
	Samskaras	Ceremonies associated with a stage in the lifecycle in Hinduism.
	Sangha	The Buddhist monastic order.
	Sawm	One of the Five Pillars of Islam; the obligation to fast during the month of Ramadan.
	Sermon	A part of the service in church when a passage from the Bible is explained.
	Sewa	The Sikh obligation to serve others.
	Shahadah	One of the Five Pillars of Islam; the statement of belief that Allah is the only God and Muhammad is Allah's messenger.
	Shema	A passage from the Jewish scriptures which underlines that God is one; used in most Jewish services.
	Shiva	One of the greatest Hindu gods.
	Shruti	'That which is remembered'; Hindu holy books remembered by holy men and written down.
	Smriti	'That which is heard'; Hindu holy books transmitted by God to men and written down.
	Stupas	Originally places where remnants of the ashes of the Buddha were buried; they have become places of pilgrimage for Buddhists.
	Sunday	The first day of the week; the Christian holy day since the fourth century.
	Synagogue	The Jewish place of worship.
T	Tallit	The Jewish prayer shawl; a four-cornered garment with fringes.
	Tefillin	Small leather boxes containing passages from the Torah, strapped on a Jewish man's arm and forehead for morning prayers on weekdays.
	Temple	The Buddhist place of worship.
	Tenakh	The name given to the Jewish scriptures.
	Ten Commandments	The ten laws which Jews believe were given to Moses by God on Mount Sinai; known by Jews as the Ten Sayings.
	Theravada Buddhists	Followers of one of two main schools of Buddhism.
	Three Jewels	The three basic beliefs of Buddhism.
	Torah	'Law' or 'teaching'; the first five books of the Jewish scriptures.
	Turban	The head-covering expected to be worn by Sikh men.
V	Varanasi	The most sacred pilgrimage destination for Hindus.
	Vihara	A Buddhist place of worship and meditation.
	Virgin Mary	Mary, the mother of Jesus; called the Virgin Mary by Roman Catholics who address prayers to her.
	Vishnu	One of the most important Hindu gods.
W	Wudu	The ritual washing routine that Muslims follow before prayer.
Z	Zakah	One of the Five Pillars of Islam; the giving $2^{1}/_{2}$ per cent of your income to help the needy.